LIGHT AND HEAVY TIMBER FRAMING MADE EAS
THOMAS HODGSON

⚒⚒ ⚒⚒ ⚒⚒ ⚒⚒ ⚒⚒ ⚒⚒ ⚒⚒ ⚒⚒

LIGHT AND HEAVY
TIMBER FRAMING
MADE EASY

Balloon Framing, Mixed Framing, Heavy
Timber Framing, Houses, Factories, Bridges,
Barns, Rinks, Timber-roofs, and all other kinds of Timber Buildings::::

Being a copious treatise on the modern practical methods of executing all kinds of timber framing, from the simple scantling shed or lean-to, to the heavy and complicated timber bridges, centers, needling and shoring, roofing and railway work, tank frames and taper structures:::::

BT

FRED T. HODGSON, F. A. I. C.

Author Op The Steel Square And Its Uses, Modern And
Practical Carpentry, Stairbuilding Made Easy, Cements,
Mortars And Stuccos, And Many Other Technical Works

Over Four Hundred and Fifty Illustrations and Diagrams

PCBLISHHRS

Frederick J. Drake & Co.

CHICAGO "U. S. *A*.

Copyright 1909

BY

FREDERICK J. DRAKE *&* CO.

Chicago

JUN 201928 INTRODUCTORY JOINTS IN WOODWORK FRAMING.

The joints shown in the following illustrations are such as are mostly employed in framed woodwork, and although they do not cover the whole ground, or show all the styles and methods of framing known to the expert workman, they include nearly all of the principal joints in general use, both in light and heavy framing; later on I may show other joints and splices that are not included in the figures shown in this portion of the work.

The introduction of steel in the construction of buildings has in a great measure displaced woodwork in the erection of large buildings in towns and cities, yet timber working is still of sufficient importance to warrant a careful study of the properties of wood and its uses, hence the following descriptions of various woods are offered in order that the worker may have a more or less intelligent idea of the nature of the materials he is manipulating.

This short treatise it is hoped will be found useful, interesting and instructive to the reader, and while it is not intended to be exhaustive, it 7 may be depended upon to be reliable as far as it goes.

All trees are divided by botanists into three classes; Exogens, or outward-growers; Endogens, or inward-growers; and Ecrogens, or summit growers—according to the relative position in which the new material for increasing the substance of the tree is added; viz., whether towards the outside, the inside or the top. Typical trees of each class would be the oak, the palm, and the tree fern. We have to deal with the exogenous class only, as that furnishes the timber in general use for construction, the term "timber" including all varieties of wood which, when felled and seasoned, are suitable for building purposes.

If the stem of an exogenous tree be cut across, it will be found to exhibit a number of nearly concentric rings, more or less distinct; and, in certain cases, radial lines intersecting them. These rings represent the annual growth of the tree which takes place just under the bark. Each ring consists of bundles of woody fibre or vascular tissue, in the form of long tapering tubes, interlaced and breaking joint with each other, having a small portion of cellular tissue at intervals. Towards the outer edge of each ring the woody fibre is harder, more compact, and of a darker color than the remaining portion. The radial lines consist of thin, hard, vertical plates formed entirely of cellular tissue, known to botanists as "Medullary rays" and to carpenters as "silver grain." Fig. 1 shows the woody fibre as seen in a magnified vertical section, Fig. 2 the cellular tissue and Fig. 3 a typical section of the stem of a young tree, *a* being the woody fibre, *b* the pith, *c* the medullary rays, and *d* the bark; the three latter consisting

Fig. 1. Fig. 2.

of cellular tissue and enclosing the woody fibre in wedge-shaped portions. As the tree advances in age, the rings and rays become more irregular, the growth being more vigorous on the sunny side, causing distortion. The strength of wood "along the grain" depends on the tenacity of the walls of the fibres and cells, while the strength "across the grain" depends on the adhesion of the sides of the tubes and cells to each other.

Tredgold proposed a classification of timber according to its mechanical structure, this, as modified by Professor Rankine which is given in the following table, also by Trantwine and others.

Class I. Pine-wood (coniferous trees—pine, fir, larch, cowrie, yew, cedar, etc.

Class II. Leaf-wood (non-coniferous trees), Division I with distinct large medullary rays.

Sub-division I. Annual rings distinct—oak.

Sub-division II. Annual rings indistinct, beech, birch, maple, sycamore, etc.

Division II. No distinct large medullary rays.

Sub-division I. Annual rings distinct—chestnut, ash, elm, etc.

Sub-division II. Annual rings indistinct—mahogany, teak, walnut, box, etc.

Knowing now the microscopical structure of the wood, we are in a position to understand the process of seasoning, and the shrinking incidental to that operation. While wood is in a growing state there is a constant passage of sap, or nutritive fluid, which keeps the whole of the interior of the tree moist

and the fibres distended, but more especially towards the outside. When the tree is cut down, and exposed to the air, the moisture gradually evaporates, causing the fibres to shrink according to certain laws; this is the natural process of seasoning. There are various methods of seasoning timber artificially, in each case the object in view is to expedite the process of evaporation. The shrinkage in length is very slight, and need not therefore be considered; but the shrinkage transversely is so great that it is necessary to look closely into the nature of it, as the question of jointing is affected considerably thereby.

If Fig. 4 be taken as representing the section of a newly felled tree, it will be seen that the wood is solid throughout, and on comparing Fig. 5 with this the result of the seasoning will be apparent. The action is exaggerated in the diagrams in order to render it more conspicuous. As the moisture evaporates, the bundles of woody fibre shrink and draw closer together; but this contraction cannot take place radially, without crushing or tearing the hard plates forming the medullary rays, which are unaffected in size by the seasoning. These plates are generally sufficiently strong to resist the crushing action, and the contraction is therefore compelled to take place in the opposite direction, *i. e.* circumferentially, the strain finding relief by splitting the timber in radial lines, allowing the medullary rays in each partially severed portion to approach each other in the same direction as the ribs of a lady's fan when closing. The illustration of a closing fan affords the best example of the principle of shrinking during seasoning, every portion of the wood practically retaining its original distance from the center. If the tree were sawn down the middle, the cut surfaces, although flat at first, would in time become rounded, as in Fig. 6, the outer portion shrinking more than that nearer the heart on account of the greater mass of woody fibre it contains and the larger amount of moisture. If cut into quarters each portion would present a similar result, as shown in Fig. 7. Figs. 8 to 12 show the same principle applied

to sawn timber of various forms, the peculiarities of which are perhaps indicated more clearly in Fig. 14. If we assume the tree to be cut into planks, as shown in Fig. 13, it will be found, after allowing due time for seasoning, that the planks have altered their shape, as in Fig. 14. Taking the center plank first, it will be observed that the thickness at the middle remains unaltered, at the edge it is reduced, and both sides are rounded, while the width remains unaltered. The planks on each side of this are rounding on the heart side, hollow on the other, retain their middle thickness, but are reduced in width in proportion to their distance from the center of the tree; or, in other words, the more nearly the annual rings are parallel to the sides of the planks the greater will be the reduction in width. The most striking result of the shrinkage is shown in Figs. 15-17. Fig. 15 shows a piece of quartering freshly cut from unseasoned timber; in Fig. 16 the part colored black shows the portion lost by shrinkage, and Fig. 17 shows the final result. These remarks apply more especially to oak, beech and the stronger firs. In the softer woods the medullary rays are more yielding, and this slightly modifies the result; but the same principles must be borne in mind if we wish to avoid the evils of shrinking which may occur from negligence in this respect.

The peculiar direction which "shakes," or natural fractures, sometimes take is due to the unequal adhesion of the woody fibres, the weakest part yielding first. In a "cup shake," which is the separation of a portion of two annual rings, the medullary rays are deficient in cohesion. This same fault sometimes occurs in white pine and has been attributed to the action of lightning and of severe frosts. So far we have considered the shrinking only as regards the cross section of various pieces. Turning now to the effect produced when we look at the timber in the other direction, Fig. 18 represents a piece of timber with the end cut off square; as this shrinks, the end remains square, the width alone being affected. If, however, the end be bevelled as in Fig. 19 we shall find that in shrinking it assumes a more acute angle, and this should be remembered in framing roofs, arranging the joints for struts, etc., especially by the carpenters who have to do actual work of fitting the parts. If the angle be an internal one or bird's mouth, it will in the same way become more acute in seasoning. The transverse shrinkage is here considered to the exclusion of any slight longitudinal alteration which might occur, and which would never be sufficient to affect the angle of the bevel. When seasoned timber is used in position subject to damp, the wood will swell in exactly the reverse direction to the shrinkage, and induce similar difficulties unless this point has also received due attention. Of course it will be seen from a study of the cross sections illustrated in the diagrams that the pieces might be selected in such a way that the shrinkage and expansion would take place chiefly in the thickness instead of the width, and thus leave the bevel unaltered. In this consists the chief art of selecting pieces for framing; but in many instances motives of economy unfortunately favor the use of pieces on stock, without reference to their suitability for the purpose required.

We may now leave the question of shrinkage, and proceed to a consideration of the more immediate intention of the book. In the following table, which shows the English method of classification, an attempt has been made to place timber tinder the different terms by which it is known, according to its size, and other accidental characteristics. This is only a rough approximation, as no definite rule can be laid down; but it may be of some assistance to those who have occasionally to deal with workmen using the terms.

Pieces larger than planks are generally called timber, but when sawn all round, are called scantling, and when sawn to equal dimensions each way, are called die-square. The dimensions (width and thickness) of parts in a framing are sometimes called the scantlings of the pieces. The term "cut stuff" is also used to distinguish wood in the state ready for the joiner, from "timber" which is wood prepared for the use of the carpenter. A "log" or "stick" is a rough whole timber unsawn.

The use of wood may be discussed under the two heads of carpentry and joinery. The former con sists principally of the use of large timbers, either rough, adzed, or sawn, and the latter of smaller pieces, always sawn, and with the exposed surfaces planed. The carpenters' work is chiefly outdoor; it embraces such objects as building timber bridges and gantries, framing roofs and floors, constructing centering, and other heavy or rough work. Joiners' work is mostly indoor; it includes laying flooring, making and fixing doors, window sashes, frames, linings, partitions, and internal fittings generally. In all oases the proper connection of the parts is an essential element, and in designing or executing joints and fastenings in woodwork, the following principles, laid down by Professor Tredgold should be adhered to viz.:— 1st. To cut the joints and arrange the fastenings so as to weaken the pieces of timber that they connect as little as possible.

2nd. To place each abutting surface in a joint as nearly as possible perpendicular to the pressure which it has to transmit. 3rd. To proportion the area of each surface to the pressure which it has to bear, so that the timber may be safe against injury under the heaviest load which occurs in practice and to form and fit every pair of such surfaces accurately in order to distribute the stress uniformly. 4th. To proportion the fastenings so that they may be of equal strength with the pieces which they connect. 5th. To place the fastenings in each piece of timber so that there shall be sufficient resistance to the giving way of the joint by the fastenings shearing or crushing their way through the timber.

To these may be added a 6th principle not less important than the foregoing, viz., To select the simplest forms of joints, and to obtain the smallest possible number of abutments. The reason for this is that the more complicated the joint, or the greater the number of bearing surfaces, the less probability there will be of getting a sound and cheaply made connection. To insure a fair and equal bearing in a joint which is not quite true, it is usual, after the pieces are put together, to run a saw cut between each bearing surface or abutment, the kerf or width of cut being equal in each case, the bearing is then rendered true. This is often done, for instance, with the shoulders of a tenon or the butting ends of a scarf, when careless workmanship has rendered it necessary. When the visible junction of two pieces is required to be as close as possible, and no great strain has to be met at the joint, it is usual to slightly undercut the parts, and give clearance on the inside, as in Fig. 20, which shows an enlarged view of a tongued and rebated heading joint in flooring. In patternmaking the fillets which are placed at the internal angle of two meeting surfaces, are made obtuse angled on the back, in order that when bradded into place the sharp edges may lie close, as shown in Fig. 21. The prints used by pattern-makers for indicating the position of round cored holes are also undercut by being turned slightly hollow on the bottom, as shown in Fig. 22. The principle is adopted in nearly all cases where a close joint is a desideratum. Clearance must also be left in joints of framing when a settlement is likely to take place, in order that after the settlement, the abutting surfaces may take a fair bearing to resist the strain.

The various strains that can come upon any member of a structure are:

Tension: Stretching or pulling,
Compression: Crushing or pushing,
Transverse Strain: Cross strain or bending,
Torsion: Twisting or wrenching,
Shearing: Cutting.

But in woodwork, when the latter force acts along the grain, it is generally called *l'* detrusion,'' the term shearing being limited to the action across the grain. The first three varieties are the strains which usually come upon ties, struts, and beams respectively. The transverse strain, it must be observed, is resolvable into tension and compression, the former occurring on the convex side of a loaded beam, and the latter on the concave side, the two being separated by the neutral axis or line of no strain. The shearing strain occurs principally in beams and is greatest at the point of support, the tendency being to cut the timber through at right angles to the grain; but in nearly all cases if the timber is strong enough to resist the transverse strain it is amply strong for any possible shearing strain which can occur. Keys and other fastenings are especially subject to shearing strain, and it will be shown in that portion of our subject that there are certain precautions to be adopted to obtain the best results.

The following tables will serve as an introduction to this portion of the subject: CLASSIFICATION OF JOINTS IN CARPENTRY,

Joints for lengthening ties, struts and beams; lapping, fishing, scarfing, tabling, building up.

Bearing-joints for beams; halving, notching, cogging, dovetailing, tusk-tenoning, housing, chasemortising.,

Joints for posts and beams; tenon, joggle, bridle, housing.

Joints for struts with ties and posts; oblique tenon, bridle, toe-joint.

Miscellaneous; butting, mitering, rebating.

CLASSIFICATION OF FASTENINGS IN CARPENTRY.
"Wedges, Nails, spikes,
  Keys, Pins, screws, bolts,
  Pins, Straps, stirrups, etc.,
  Wood pins, Sockets,
And for joinery must be added glue.

We will consider these joints in the order given above. One of the first requirements in the use of timber for engineering purposes is the connection of two or more beams to obtain a greater length. Fig. 23 shows the method of lengthening a beam by lapping another to it, the two being held together by straps and prevented from sliding by the insertion of keys. Fig. 24 shows a similar joint, through-bolts being used instead of straps, and wrought-iron plates instead of oak keys. This makes a neater joint than the former, but they are both unsightly and whenever adopted 23 the beams should be arranged in three or five pieces in order that the supports at

each end may be level and the beams horizontal. This joint is more suitable for a cross strain than for tension and compression. Fig. 25 shows the common form of a finished beam adapted for compression. If required to resist tensile strain, keys should be inserted in the top and bottom joints between the bolts. Fig. 26 shows a fished joint adapted for a cross strain, the whole sectional area of the original beam taking the compressive portion of the cross strain, and the fishing piece taking the tensile portion. Fig. 27 shows a fished beam for the same purpose in which a wrought-iron plate turned up at the ends takes the tensile strain. Tabling consists of bedding portions of one beam into the other longitudinally. Occasionally the fishing pieces are tabled at the ends into the beams to resist the tendency to slip under strain, but this office is better performed by keys, and in practice tabling is not much used. The distinction between fished beams and scarfed beams is that in the former

I
"tst o ©
Fig. 27.

the original length is not reduced, the pieces being butted against each other, while in the latter the beams themselves are cut in a special manner and lapped partly over each other; in both cases additional pieces of wood or iron are attached to strengthen the joint. Fig. 28 shows a form of scarf adapted to short posts. Here the scarf is cut square and parallel to the sides, so that the full sectional area is utilized for resisting the compressive strain. When the post is longer and liable to a bending strain the scarf should be inclined, as in Fig. 29, to allow of greater thickness being retained at the shoulder of each piece, the shoulder being kept square. In this joint a considerable strain may be thrown on the bolts from the sliding tendency of the scarf, if the shoulders should happen to be badly fitted, as any slipping would virtually increase the thickness of the timber where the bolts pass through. The width of each shoulder should be not less than one-fourth the total thickness. Joints in posts are mostly re quired

when it is desired to lengthen piles already driven, to-support a superstructure in the manner of columns. Another form of scarf for a post put together without bolts is shown in Fig. 30, the parts being tabled and tongued, and held together by wedges. This is not a satisfactory joint, and i3 moreover, expensive because of its requiring extra care in fitting; but it may be a suitable joint in some special cases, in which all the sides are re quired to be flush. Fig. 31 shows the common form of scarf in a tie-beam. The ends of the scarf are bird's mouthed, and the joint is tightened up bywedges driven from opposite sides. It is further secured by the wrought-iron plates on the top and bottom, which are attached to the timber by bolts and nuts. In all these joints the friction between the surfaces, due to the bolts being tightly screwed up, plays an important part in the strength of the joint; and as all timber is liable to shrink, it is

Fig. 33.

necessary to examine the bolts occasionally, and to keep them well tightened up. Figs. 32 and 33 show good forms of scarfs, which are stronger but not so common as the preceding. Sometimes the scarf is made vertically instead of horizontally, and when this is done a slight modification is made in the position of the projecting tongue, as will be seen from Fig. 34, which shows the joint in ele vation and plan. The only other scarfs to which attention need be called are those shown in Figs. 35 and 36 in which the compression side is made with a square abutment. These are very strong formsj at the same time easily made. Many other forms have been designed, and old books on carpentry teem with scarfs of every conceivable pattern; but in this, as in many other cases, the simplest thing is the best, as the whole value depends upon the accuracy of the workmanship, and this is rendered excessively difficult with a multiplicity of parts or abutments.

In building up beams to obtain increased strength the most usual method is to lay two together sideways for short spans, as in the lintels over doors and windows, or to cut one down the middle and reverse the halves, inserting a wrought iron plate between, as shown in the flitch-girder, Fig. 37. The reversal of the halves gives no additional strength, as many workmen suppose, but it enables one to see if the timber is sound throughout to the heart, and it also allows the pieces to season better. A beam uncut may be decayed in the center, and hence the advantage of cutting and reversing, even if no flitch-plate is to be inserted, defective pieces being then discarded. When very long and strong beams are required, a simple method is to bolt several together so as to break joint with each other, as shown in Fig. 38, taking care that on the tension side the middle of one piece comes in the center of the stand with the two nearest joints equidistant. It is not necessary in a built beam to carry the full depth as far as the supports; the strain is, of course, greatest in the center, and provided there is sufficient depth given at that point, the beam may be reduced towards the ends, allowance being made for the loss of strength at the joints on tension side. A single piece of timber secured to the underside of a beam at the center, as in Fig. 39 is a simple and effective mode of increasing its strength. It will be observed that the straps are bedded into the sides of the beams; they thus form keys to prevent the pieces from slipping on each other. This weakens the timber much less than cutting out the top or bottom, as the strength of a beam varies not only in direct proportion to the breadth, but as the square of the depth. The addition of a second piece of timber in the middle is a method frequently adopted for strengthening shear legs and derrick poles temporarily for lifting heavy weights.

We now come to the consideration of bearing joints for beams, the term "beam" being taken to include all pieces which carry or receive a load across the grain. The simplest of these is the halving joint, shown at Fig. 40, where two pieces of cross bracing are halved together. This joint is also shown at Fig. 41, where the ends of two wall plates

meet each other. "When a joint occurs in the length of a beam, as at Fig. 42, it is generally called a scarf. In each of these examples it will be seen that half the thickness of each piece is cut away so as to make the joint flush top and bottom. Sometimes the outer end of the upper piece is made thicker, forming a bevelled joint and acting as a dovetail when loaded on top. This is shown at Figs. 43 and 44. When one beam crosses another at right angles, and is cut on the lower side to fit upon it, the joint is known as single notching, shown in Fig. 45. When both are cut, as in Fig.

Fig. 47.

46, it is known as double notching. These forms occur in the bridging and ceiling joists shown on the diagrams of double and double-framed flooring. When a cog or solid projecting portion is left in the lower piece at the middle of the joint it is known as cogging, cocking, or caulking, and is shown in Fig. 47. Figs. 48 and 49 show two forms of the joint occurring between a tie-beam and wall plate in roofing. Dove-tailing is not much used in carpentry or house-joinery, owing to the shrinkage of the wood loosening the joint. Two wall plates are shown dovetailed together at Figs. 50 and 51; in the latter a wedge is sometimes in

Fig. 50.

serted on the straight side to enable the joint to be tightened up as the wood shrinks. Tredgold proposed the form shown in Fig. 52 which is known as the "Tredgold notch"; but this is never seen in practice. Tusk-tenoning is the method adopted for obtaining a bearing for one beam meeting another at right angles at the same level. Fig. 53 shows a trimmer supported on a trimming joist in this manner; this occurs round fire-places, hoistways, and other openings through floors. Fig. 54 shows the same joint between a wood girder and binding joist, it is also seen in the diagram of double-framed flooring. The advantage of this form is that a good bearing is obtained without, weakening the beam to any very great extent, as the principal portion of the material removed is taken from the neutral axis, leaving the re-

mainder disposed somewhat after the form of a flanged girder. "When a cross piece of timber has to be framed in between two beams already fixed, a tenon and chase-mortise (Fig. 55), is one of the methods adopted. If the space is very confined, the same kind of mortise is made in both beams, but in opposite directions; the cross piece is then held obliquely, and slid into place. Occasionally it is necessary to make the chase-mortise vertical, but this is not to be recommended, as the beam is more weakened by so doing—it is shown in Fig. 56. Ceiling joists, fixed by tenons and chase-mortises, are shown on the diagram of double flooring. In sorie *vases,* a square fillet is nailed on, as shown in the same diagram, to take the weight of the joists without cutting into the beam. While speaking of floors, the process of furring-up may be mentioned; this consists of laying thin pieces, or strips, of wood on the top of joists, or any surfaces, to bring them up to a level. Furring-pieces are also sometimes nailed underneath the large beams in framed floors, so that the under side may be level with the bottom of the ceiling joists, to give a bearing for the laths, and at the same time allow sufficient space for the plaster to form a key. Brandering is formed by strips about one inch square, nailed to the under side of the ceiling joists at right angles to them; these strips help to stiffen the ceiling, and being narrower than the ceiling joists, do not interrupt the key of the plastering so much—this is also shown on the diagram of double flooring. Housing consists of letting one piece of wood bodily into another for a short distance, or, as it were, a tenon the full size of the stuff. This is shown in the diagram of staircase details, where the treads and risers are seen housed into the strings, and held by wedges. Housing is likewise adopted for fixing rails to posts, as in Fig. 57, where an arris rail is shown housed into an oak post for fencing. The most common joint, however, between posts and beams, is the tenon and mortise joint, either wedged or fixed by a pin; the former arrangement is shown in Fig. 58, and the latter in Fig. 59. The friction of the wedges, when tightly driven, aided by the adhesion of the glue or white lead with which they are coated, forms, in effect, a solid dovetail, and the fibres being compressed, do not yield further by the shrinking of the wood. In the diagram of a framed door will be seen an example of the application of this joint and in the adjacent diagram will be seen the evils produced by careless fitting, or the use of unseasoned material. When it is desired to tenon a beam into a post, without allowing the tenon to show through, or where a mortise has to be made in an existing post fixed against a wall, the dovetail tenon, shown in Fig. 60 is sometimes adopted, a wedge being driven in on the straight side to draw the tenon home and keep it in place. In joining small pieces, the foxtail tenon, shown in Fig. 61 has the same advantage as the dovetail tenon, of not showing through; but it is more difficult to fix. The outer wedges are made the longest, and in driving the tenon home, these come into action first, splitting away the sides, and filling up the dovetail mortise, at the same time compressing the fibres of the tenon. This joint requires no glue, as it cannot draw out; should it work loose at any time, the only way to tighten it up would be to insert a very thin wedge in one end of the mortise. Short tenons, assisted by strap bolts, as shown in Fig. 62 are commonly adopted in connecting large timbers. The post is cut to form a shoulder so that the beam takes a bearing for its full width, the tenon preventing any side movement. When a post rests on a beam or sill piece, its movement is prevented by a "joggle," or stub-tenon, as shown in Fig. 63; but too much reliance should not be placed on this tenon, owing to the impossibility of seeing, after the pieces are fixed, whether it has been properly fitted, and it is particularly liable to decay from moisture settling in the joint. For temporary purposes, posts are commonly secured to heads and sills by dog-irons, or "dogs," Fig. 64; the pieces in this case simply butt against each other, the object being to avoid cutting the timber, and so depreciating its value, and also for economy of labor. Other forms of tenons are shown in Figs. 65 and 66. The double tenon is used in framing wide pieces, and the haunched tenon when the edge of the piece on which the tenon is formed is required to be flush with the end of the piece containing the mortise. Examples of both these will be found in the diagram of framed door. In Figs. 67 and 68 are shown two forms of bridle joint between a post and a beam. Tredgold and Hatfield recommended a bridle joint with a circular abut ment, but this is not a correct form, as the post is then equivalent to a column with rounded ends, which it is well known is unable in that form to

Fig. 69.

bear so great a load before it commences to yield. A strut meeting a tie, as in the case of the foot of a principal rafter in a roof truss, is generally tenoned into the tie by an oblique tenon, as shown in Fig. 69; and the joint is further strengthened by a toe on the rafter bearing against a shoulder in the tie. Tredgold strongly advised this joint being made with a bridge instead of a tenon, as shown in Fig. 70, on account of the abutting surfaces being fully open to view. A strut meeting a post as in Fig. 71, or a strut meeting the principal rafter of a roof-truss (Fig. 72) is usually connected by a simple toe-joint. The shoulder should be cut square with the piece containing it, or it should bisect the angle formed between the two pieces. It is sometimes made square with the strut, but this is incorrect, as there would in some cases be a possibility of the pieces lipping out. In battoned and braced doors or gates this joint is used, the pieces being so arranged as to form triangles, and so prevent the liability to sag or drop, which is so difficult to guard against in square framed work without struts or braces. When a structure is triangulated, its shape remains constant so long as the fastenings are not torn away, because, with a given length of sides, a triangle can assume only one position; but this is not the case with foursided framing, as the sides, while remaining constant in length may vary in position. The diagram of a mansard roof shows various examples of a toe-joint; it shows also the principal framing kingpost and queen-post roof trusses, each portion being triangulated to insure the utmost stability. *I* B I

Fig. 74.

Fig. 75.

m

Fig. 73.

Among the miscellaneous joints in carpentry not previously mentioned the most common are the butt joint, Fig. 73, where the pieces meet each other with square ends or sides; the mitre joint, Fig. 74, where the pieces abut against each other with bevelled ends, bisecting the angle between them, as in the case of struts mitered to a corbel piece supporting the beam of a gantry; and the rabbeted or "rebated" joint, Fig. 75, which is a kind of narrow halving, either transverse or longitudinal. To these must be added in joinery the grooved and tongued joint, Fig. 76, the matched and beaded joint, Fig. 77, the dowelled joint, Fig. 78, the dovetailed joint, Fig. 79, and other modifications of these to suit special purposes. The application of several of these joints is shown on the various diagrams of flooring, etc. To one of these it may be desirable to" call particular attention, viz.: the flooring laid folding. This is a method of obtaining close joints without the use of a cramp. It consists of nailing down two boards and leaving a space between them rather less than the width of, say five boards, these boards are then put in place, and the two projecting edges are forced down by laying a plank across them, and standing on it. This may generally be detected in old floors by observing that several heading joints come in one line, as shown on the diagram, instead of breaking joint with each other. It is worthy of notice that the tongue, or slip feather, shown in Fig. 76, which in good work is formed generally of hard wood, is made up of short pieces cut diagonally across the grain of the plank, in order that any movement of the joints may not split the tongue, which would inevitably occur if it were cut longitudinally from the plank.

With regard to fastenings, the figures already given show several applications. Wedges should be split or torn from the log, so that the grain may be continuous, or if sawn out, a straight-grained piece should be selected. Sufficient taper should be put on to give enough compression to the joint, but too much taper would allow the possibility of the wedge working loose. For outside work, wedges should be painted over with white lead before being driven, this not being affected by moisture, as glue would be. In scarf-joints the chief use of wedges is to draw the parts together before the bolt-holes are bored. Keys are nearly parallel strips of hard wood or metal; they are usually made with a slight draft to enable them to fit tightly. If the key is cut lengthwise of the grain, a piece with curled or twisted grain should be selected, but if this cannot be done, the key should be cut crossways of the log from which it is taken, and inserted in the joint with the grain at right angles to the direction of the strain, so that the shearing stress to which the key is subject may act upon it across the fibres. In timber bridges and other large structures cast iron keys are frequently used, as there is with them an absence of all difficulty from shrinkage. Wood pins should be selected in same way as wedges, from straightgrained, hard wood. Square pins are more efficient than round pins, but are not often used, on account of the difficulty of forming square holes for their reception. Tenons are frequently secured in mortises, as in Fig. 59, by pins, the pins being driven in such a manner as to draw the tenon tightly into the mortise up to its shoulders, and afterwards to hold it there. This is done by boring the hole first through the cheeks of the mortise, then inserting the tenon, marking off the position of the hole, removing the tenon, and boring the pinhole in it rather nearer the shoulders than the mark, so that when the pin is driven it will draw the tenon as above described. This method is called "drawboring." The dowelled floor shown in Fig. 78 gives another example of the use of pins.

Nails, and their uses, are too well known to need description; it may, however, be well to call attention to the two kinds of cut and wrought nails, the former being sheared or stamped out of plates,. and the latter forged out of rods. The cut nails are cheaper, but are rather brittle; they are useful in many kinds of work, as they may be driven without previously boring holes to receive them, being rather blunt pointed and having two parallel sides, which are placed in the direction of the grain of the wood. The wrought nails do not easily break, and are used where it is desired to clench them on the back to draw and hold the wood together. The following table gives the result of some experiments on the adhesion of nails and screws.

French, or wire nails have almost driven the cut and wrought nails out of the market. Wire nails, however, are not as lasting as the old fashioned ones, but they are clean, handy to work and can be clinched whenever necessary. They rust quickly, and should not be used for shingling or where damp is likely to get to them.

SUMMARY.

Across Grain. With Grain. Adhesion of nails in Pine....2 to 1 Adhesion of nails in Elm....4 to 3

Entrance to extraction is as 6 to 5.

Common screw.2" diam. equals 3 times the adhesive force of a six-penny nail.

Spikes are nearly of the same form as nails, but much larger and are mostly used for heavy timber work. Treenails, so-called, are hard wood pins used in the same way as nails. In particular work, with some woods, such as Oak, they are used to prevent the staining of the wood, which would occur if nails were used and any moisture afterwards reached them. Compressed treenails are largely used in England for fixing railway chairs to sleepers as they swell on exposure to moisture, and then hold more firmly. Screws are used in situations where the parts may afterwards require to be disconnected. They are more useful than nails, as they not only connect the parts, but draw them closer together, and are more secure. For joiner's work the screws usually have countersunk heads; where it is desired to conceal them, they are let well into the wood, and the holes plugged with dowels of the same kind of wood, with the grain in the same direction. For carpenters' work the screws are larger and have often square heads; these are known as coach-screws. The bolts, nuts, and washers used in carpentry may be of the proportions given in the following table:—an example is shown in Fig. 80.

Thickness of nut 1 diam. of bolt

Thickness of head ⅝ diam. of bolt

Diam. of head or nut over sides.1⅝ diam. of bolt Side of square washer for fir..3 1/2 diam. of bolt Side of square washer for oak.2⅝ diam. of bolt Thickness of washer $y2$ diam. of bolt

The square nuts used by carpenters are generally much too thin; unless they are equal in thickness to the diameter of the bolt, the full advantage of that diameter cannot be obtained, the strength of any connection being measured by its weakest part. The best proportion for nuts is shown in the diagram of a standard hexagon nut. A large square washer is generally put under the nut to prevent it from sinking into the wood and tearing the fibres while being screwed up, but it is also necessary to put on a similar washer under the head to prevent sinking into the wood. This is, however, often improperly omitted. Straps are bands of wrought-iron placed over a joint to strengthen it and tie the parts together. When the strap is carried round one piece, and both ends secured to a piece joining it at right angles, as in a king-post and tie-beam, it is known as a stirrup, and is tightened by means of a cotter and gib-keys as shown in Fig. 81. When straps connect more than two pieces of timber together, they are made with a branch leading in the direction of each piece; but they are usually not strong enough at the point of junction, and might often be made shorter than they are without impairing their efficiency. Sockets are generally of cast-iron, and may be described as hollow boxes formed to receive the ends of timber framing.

With regard to the use of glue for securing joints, it has been found that the tensile strength of solid glue is about 4,000 lbs. per square inch, while that of a glued joint in damp weather is from 350 to 360 lbs. per square inch, and in dry weather about 715 lbs. per square inch. The lateral cohesion of pine wood is about 562 lbs. per square inch, and therefore in a good glue joint the solid material will give way before the junction yields.

These joints, though quite numerous, do not exhibit all that are used in carpentry and joinery, but are quite sufficient for our present purpose, as others will be illustrated and described as we proceed.

In balloon or scantling buildings of all kinds, good solid foundations should in every case be provided, for most of the defects often found in frame buildings such as cracks, breaks, sags, etc. are in a great measure due to the settlement of foundation walls, pins, posts or undue shrinkage. When possible, all wood materials such as studding, joists, rafters, collar-beams, trimmers, sills, plates, braces and all other timber or lumber used, should be well seasoned, particularly the joists, as the shrinking of the joists causes the partitions to drop and this makes cracks in the angles of the walls, causes the doors to drag on the floors or to bind at the top and thus disarrange the locks, bolts, catches or other fastenings. Shrinkage of wall studs causes trouble around the windows and outside doors, leaving openings for wind to make its way through into the interior of the house. These things, though apparently of little moment, are quite necessary to be taken into consideration if a good warm and substantial building is de' sired.

We are now ready to undertake some examples of real work. The first thing to be considered when preparing for a balloon frame after the foundation wall is ready to put on the frame work, is the sill on which the studding is to stand. Of these there are many kinds and I propose to illustrate a selection from which the builder may choose the one most suitable to his purpose. Fig. 82 is about the most simple of any and is nothing more or less than a 2x4-inch scantling halved at the corner, and may be fastened by a wooden pin or nailed together as shown. A sill of this kind should be laid in mortar and levelled up to take the joists and studding. The joists in this case will rest on the sill altogether, as shown in Fig. 83 or they may be cut or "checked" so as to rest both on stone wall and sill. Fig. 84 shows another method of forming a sill in the old fashioned way. This makes a good strong sill and secures a warm connection between sill and wall. Another good plan is shown at Fig. 85. Figs. 86, 87, 88, 89, 90 and 91 show a number of various methods of forming sills all of which are good. All sills of this kind should be bedded in mortar and levelled up on their top flats, and when convenient the spaces between the joists on the wall should be filled in with stone or brickwork level with the top of the upper edges of the joists. By doing this, the building is made more comfortable, stronger, and vermin of all kinds will be prevented from getting into the build ing, and the joists are held together solid in their places. Of course the stone or brick work must "be laid in mortar and well flushed up.

Sometimes balloon frames are built up on timber sills of various dimensions and it may be well to give a few examples here of this method, although the matter of framing and laying the sills is simple enough.

Some timber varies in size, often from onefourth to one-half an inch, and in framing the corners this fact must be noted and provided for or the studs will be too long or too short as the case may be, and the joists will not be in line on top. The sills should be all sized to the same dimension, and all joists should be «ized and made equal in width. Fig. 92 exhibits one method of using a timber sill. This is rather a troublesome method and costly, but is really an excellent way as it gives a bearing to the edge of the joists both on the sill and on the stonework. At Fig. 93 we show another method of using a timber sill. Sometimes, in cases of this kind a tenon is worked on the end of the joists and a corresponding mortise is made in the sill to receive it; more frequently, however, the ends of the joists are nailed to the sill by be ing toe-nailed to it. This method of using a timber sill is not to be recommended, but when it is employed it is always better to cut in boards tight between the joists and nail the boards solid to the sill. This makes a fair job and insures the joists staying in their places. Another method, with a part of the studded wall—in section—is shown in Fig. 94. This illustration also shows the second and third joists and their manner of attachment to the wall studs. The rafter and scheme for forming the cornice are shown so that the diagram may be followed by the workman without trouble. Fig. 95 shows another example of heavy sill with a portion of the wall at the corner and at one side of a window opening. It will be noticed that the corner stud and the jamb stud at the window are made 4x4 inches in section. Where such studs can be obtained it is best to get them solid, but the usual way of forming these corners, is to nail two studs together which answer the purpose very well. The joists are notched or checked onto a 2"x4" scantling which is spiked to lower edge of the sill to receive the joists. This is not a good way unless the lower edges of the joists rests on the stonework as shown in Figs. 92 and 93, as the joists are apt to split at the comer of the notching if a heavier weight happens to be placed on the floor than was at first intended. The old-fashioned way of framing a heavy sill to receive joists is shown in Fig. 96. This method now is almost obsolete and is only used where joists are to be carried across a large room and

Fig. 96.

where a beam or bearer is not admissible as nothing must show in the room below the ceiling, and where joists are in two lengths. It will be noticed that there are three different methods of framing the joists in the sill. The first shows the mortise too low down on the sill, the second too high up, while the third is in the strongest point where a single tenon and mortise are employed.

In the top of the sill the stud mortises are shown, with two studs *in situ* and one out to show the tenon. There were various methods of framing the joists into the sills in order to obtain the greatest resistance to pressure, among which was the double tenon, the tusk tenon, such as shown in Fig. 97, the upper example being disengaged and the lower one in place. There are also many other methods of framing joists into heavy timber sills, but I have exhibited sufficient examples to give an idea of the general methods, and when we get to heavy framing, I will say more on the subject and offer a few extra examples. Fig 98 shows another oldtime method of framing a sill. This is called "Gaining and mortising a sill," and was often put in specifications under this term. Fig. 99 shows a method of forming a sill called a "box sill," as a matter of fact it is no sill at all, being formed of two joists. It is simple,' however, and is fairly effective. Another box sill is shown at Fig. 100. This is often used where there is a good foundation under it, it makes a very good sill, when the studding is cut so as to go down to the bottom and occasionally when spiked in the joist as well as the sill it makes a very strong job.

Fig. 101 is another strong way which can be con structed a little quicker and is good for a cheap job, but I prefer the other. Fig. 102 is cheaper-still and used a good deal, just the one piece laid flat on the wall, the joist put on and a 2x4 nailed on the joist, and then the studding nailed to that. Or let the studding run down to the sill and do away with the 2x4 on the joist.

In f orming partitions and walls in balloon and scantling buildings much care is required in arranging the studding at the corners and about the doors and windows in order to get the best results with as little expenditure of materials and labor as possible, and in order to aid the workman in this direction, I have gathered together from various sources a number of examples, the very best obtainable for this purpose and embody them in this department. Take for instance the corner posts in a balloon

frame where it has to serve for receiving the finishing materials—board ing and lathing—on both its inner and outer angles. These should be straight, firm and solid, and constructed so as to make a good outside and inside corner. Fig. 103 shows a substantial way, simply by nailing four together strong with a good outside and nice inside corner to lath on. Fig. 104 is another way practically as good and saves one studding. But if the thickness of two was not the width of one it would bother a little.

Fig. 105 is a method of nailing together the corner studding in a way to avoid the difficulty just mentioned and makes a good corner.

Fig. 106 shows how a good corner for a cheap job can be made with two studding; if the building is not sheathed a five-inch corner board nailed together at the corner works alright, and chamfered on the corner looks well, too. Of course, if there was to be a quarter round in the corner that corner shown would not do at all. I think you all have a corner on that subject and now we will mention partitions. Fig. 107 shows that where the cross partition comes, the studding should be 3 inches (not 4) apart, and then spike the cross partition studding to them and you have a solid corner that the plastering will have no excuse to crack in. Fig. 108 shows corner of partition where the par tition is put up the 2-inch way, as they often are in closets and light work. If you wish the building to show as high as possible on the outside and not have the ceiling too high on the inside, Fig. 109 shows a good method for plate and ceiling joists; for better job the plates could be doubled. Fig. 110 shows a double plate ceiling joist on top corner, cut to keep from projecting above rafter, which makes the best job for general purposes.

At Fig. Ill I show two other corners sometimes used. One of these shows the least amount of material that can be used for an outer corner while the other one shows a solid corner formed with four pieces and is similar to Fig. 103, and the other to Fig. 107. At Fig. 112 is shown two examples, the upper one is for the starting point of a partition,

the lower one shows the double stud to be used for the jamb studs for windows and doors. Fig. 113 shows the proper method of running lath behind a partition wall, X showing the stud starting the partition. This is not a good method, though very often made use of, as the angles are likely to crack. A much better way is shown at Fig. 114, which, if adopted, and done well will prevent the plaster from cracking. The 2x3inch piece indicated by A in Fig. 114 should be out in every 2 feet in height of partition and well nailed, especially to the 2x5-inch B. When 2x3inch studding is used in the main partition we would suggest employing lx5-inch piece B, instead

Fig. 113.

of a 2x5-inch. Fig. 115 shows a section of a wall intended for a house having two stories, a cellar and attic. This shows the sill, cellar wall and rafters of additional annex, the annex being only one story and cellar. Another sectional view of outside wall with inside and outside finish is shown at Fig. 116. This shows the manner of forming the sill, placing in window headers, cornice and general finish. As this section is drawn to a scale of half-inch to the foot, it may be worked from if desired. Another section of an outside wall of a simpler kind is shown at Fig. 117. This is for a one and a half story house, finished quite plainly inside and out.

In setting up inside partitions more care and attention than is usually paid to the openings should be given. A careless haphazard way of trimming the heads of doorways and the consequent result after a few years, is shown at Fig. 118. This figure, of course, shows the condition in an exaggerated form, but the condition does often occur very much to the detriment of the door and its trimmings. Fig. 119 shows a good oldfashioned way of framing a door head so that no movement or distortion like that shown in 118 can possibly take place as the braces at the head are toed, or notched, into the top stretcher which prevents them from pressing out the jamb studs. Another method which is quite common, and which should be avoided, is shown in Fig. 120. This last is a cheap slip-shod way of fixing partitions over doors but it very often leads to trouble after the building is occupied, and it should be avoided in the interests of good and permanent work. The difference in cost between building a doorway as at Fig. 120 and Fig. 119 is so small that no contractor should for a moment hesitate in adopting the better plan. The sill, or girder and joist shown in Fig. 119 need not be followed, they are exhibited just to show the old methods of doing good substantial work and may yet be employed in some situations. At Fig. 124, I show a portion of a floor with the end of the joist resting on a bond timber which is supported on a ledge formed in the brick wall by making the upper story one half a brick thinner than the wall below. This is a very good way to carry the joists when it can be accomplished without injury to the wall and where the building is not more than three stories in height. Fig. 125 shows a section of a floor with joists, floor, ceiling and cross bridging. This is a good example of building a good solid floor for all ordinary purposes. i

Fig. 126 shows cross bridging with floor or ceiling and Fig. 127 exhibits the proper way to cut in the joists in a brick wall where it is necessary to run the joists in the brick wall. The joists should rest on a timber which is built in the wall as the bricks are laid.

A good way to set up second or third-story studs is shown at Fig. 128. Of course, where the studding can be obtained long enough to run the whole height of the building it is better to get them if the cost will admit, if not, the method shown will answer very well. Fig. 129 shows a good method of trussing a partition, it is simple and can be done without much labor and is quite effective.

At Fig. 130 I show a method of preparing a wall of scantling for veneering with brick; it is simple and does not require much skill to make a good wall. The proper way is to put down a stone foundation wall of sufficient thickness to carry both framing and brick wall,

as shown at Fig. 130. The brickwork is tied every sixth course with proper anchors, as shown, which are about 6 inches long, and which are nailed to the sides of the studs. The studding may be 2x4 or 2x6 inches, and framed in the ordinary manner. It is considered the better way to rough board the outside of the studding and then cover the boarding with good building paper, and brick against this. A good warm job is the result if the work is properly done. The bricks are all well laid as "stretchers" when done this way, and the best bricks should be selected for the work. At this point it may not be out of place to show some of the methods of laying down joists and securing hearth and stair trimmers, and other similar work. As I have shown in Fig. 127, all joists entering in a wall should be cut with bevel ends, so that in case of fire and the joists being burned or broken in or about their centers, then should they fall down, they would pry out either the bricks or stone above them and thus tend to destroy the wall. The employment of bridging as shown in Figs. 125 and 126 is for the purpose of stiffening the joists by keeping them from twisting, and distributing the strain over a larger number of joists than those on which the weight comes. The bridge piers should be 2x2 inches, though 1x2 are frequently used, and they should be accurately cut to the required angle and firmly nailed. A good way to find the lengths and bevels of the pieces required for the braces is to snap a chalked line across the top edges of the joists, parallel with the side of the wall, and a second line distant from the first, just the depth of joists, and of course, parallel to the first line. The length and angle of the braces can then be obtained by laying the piece diagonally on the joists, with its edges just touching the chalk lines on the inner edge of both joists, keeping the thickness of the stuff inside the two lines. In this position mark the underside of the bridge piece with a pencil, and both the proper angles and right length are given. Each piece obtained this way answers for the second piece in the same space. Two nails should be driven in each end

of the bridge piece, if a good permanent job is desired.

In trimming around a chimney or a stair wellhole, several methods are employed. Sometimes the header and trimmers are made from material twice as thick and the same depths as the ordinary joists, and the intermediate joists are tenoned into the header, as shown in Figs. 131 and 132. Here we have T, T, for header, and T, J, T, J, for trimmers, and b, j, for the ordinary joists. In the western and also some of the central states, the trimmers and headers are made up of two thicknesses of the header being mortised to secure the ends of the joists. The two thicknesses are well nailed together; this method is exhibited at Fig. 133, which also shows one way to trim around the hearth; C, C, C, C, shows the header with tusk tenons on ends, which pass through the trimmers A, A.

At Fig. 134 I show another scheme for trimming around a fireplace in which the trimmers and leaders T, T, are seen, the headers being tenoned through the trimmer joists with tusk tenons and keyed solid in place. The central line of hearth is seen at X Y, the intermediate joists at b j and the trimmers at t j, while the bond timbers are in evidence at w p. Here there are two flues shown, also the hearth tiling. In this example there are two holding bolts shown by dotted lines on each side of the fireplace anchored into the brick-wall and passing under the hearth and through the header to which it is secured with a nut and washer. A dump grate is shown at s s. This is for the purpose of letting ashes down a shute into the cellar where there should be an iron receptacle to receive them.

Fig. 134.

Fig. 135 shows a sectional view of the hearth X Y, of Fig. 134. This shows a brick arch turned under the hearth to support it, the center for which the carpenter is expected to make. There is an oak or other suitable hardwood strip mitred around the tiles and of the same thickness as the flooring. The flooring is shown at b, and the joists and trimmer are shown at b j and t j, respectively; the dump shute is shown at the shaded part and may continue to cellar floor, or cut through the wall at any desirable point convenient to remove ashes.

In ordinary buildings the brick arch is seldom employed, the header being placed pretty close to the brick work and the joists tenoned into it, and the tops of the joists being cut down enough to allow a layer of concrete cement and tiles on the top of them without raising the tiles above the floor. In such cases strips are nailed to the sides of the joists, three or four inches below the top of the cut joists. Rough boards are then laid in these strips after which the space is filled in with coarse mortar to the level of top edges of joists, then the concrete cement and tiles are laid on this, which makes the hearth pretty safe from taking fire and brings the tiles to the floor level; where it may not be considered safe to trim down the joists to this requirement, the joists may be beveled on their top edges saw-tooth shape, and this will serve the purpose nearly as well as cutting them down below their top edges three or four inches.

Frequently it happens that a chimney rises in a building from its own foundation, disconnected from the walls, in which case the chimney shaft will require to be trimmed all around as shown in Fig. 133. In cases of this kind the trimmers A, A, should be made of stuff very much thicker than the joists, as they have to bear a double burden, B, B, shows the heading, and C, C, C, C, the tail joists. B, B, should have a thickness double that of C, C, etc., and A, A, should at least be three times as stout as C, C, this will to some extent equalize the strength of the whole floor, which is a matter to be considered in laying down floor timbers, for a floor is no stronger than its weakest part.

There are a number of devices for trimming around stairs, fireplaces and chimney stacks by which the cutting or mortising of the timbers is avoided. One method is to cut the timbers the exact length, square in the ends, and then insert iron dowels—two or more—in the ends of the joists, and boring holes in the trimmers and headers to suit and dri-

ving the whole solid together. The dowels are made from ⅝ to 1" round iron. Another and better device is the "bridle iron," which may be hooked over the trimmer or header, as the case may be, the stirrup carrying the abutting timber, as shown in Fig. 136. These

"bridle irons" are made of wrought iron, $2x2y2$ inches or larger dimensions if the work requires such; for ordinary jobs, however, the size given will be found plenty heavy for carrying the tail joists, and a little heavier may be employed to carry the header. This style of connecting the trimmings does not hold the frame work together, and in places where there is any tendency to thrust the work apart, some provision must be made to prevent the work from spreading. This may readily be done in many ways that will suggest themselves to the workman. Perhaps the best way is to nail a hoop iron across the points lapping one end up the side of the trimmer or header, and bending it over the arris, running it along the edge of the joists across the joints, and extending it beyond the joints ten or twelve inches.

In no case where a trimmer or header is placed alongside a chimney stack should the woodwork be less than $iy2$ inches from the brickwork. This is a precaution taken to prevent the heat of the stack from setting fire to the timbers; the flooring of course is obliged to be within one inch of the brickwork, but the bare board always covers the joint.

I show a few examples of trimming around a fireplace or chimney. Fig. 137 shows a very good way, and one very frequently employed. Another way, and one deserving of consideration is shown in Fig. 138. The ends of the stretchers enter the brick wall of the chimney, into which has been inserted cast-iron shoes to receive them. These shoes prevent sparks or fire from reaching the timbers from the flue and make them secure against burning. At Fig. 139 I show a trimmer with double mortises, also notches in the ends of the stretchers. These notches are to fit over a raised rib of iron in the cast-iron shoes, I show in Fig. 138. Notches are sometimes cut in the stretchers, to fit over a bar of

iron which is sometimes used to carry joists over an opening where joists cannot be let into the brick wall, as shown at Fig. 140. This also shows how joists may be carried over small openings by making use of a flat iron bar which has screw bolts run through them to carry the joists below. Where a girder or timber is used to carry joists it is sometimes necessary to drop the timbers two inches, thereby affording greater strength in the beam, but with the disadvantage of projecting below the ceiling. Fig. 141 shows the proper proportions for framing the end of the joists. In trimming for a chimney in a roof the "headers," "stretchers" or "trimmers" and "tail rafters" may be simply nailed in place, as there is no great weight beyond snow and wind pressure to carry, therefore the same precautions for strength are not necessary. The sketch shown at Fig. 142 explains how the chimney opening in the roof may be trimmed—the parts being only spiked together. A shows a hip rafter against which the cripples or jacks, on both sides are spiked. The chimney stack is shown in the center of the roof—isolated—trimmed on the four sides. The sketch is self-explanatory in a measure and should be easily understood.

"We may now venture to build a small house and finish same on the lines laid down, that is to say, a balloon frame house. We already know enough to raise the walls, put up and complete partitions and trim and finish openings. Suppose our building to be 24x42 feet on the ground. This should be laid off as shown in Fig. 143, first the foundation, then the first floor as shown, then the second floor with three bed-rooms, hall and closets. The manner of laying the joists is shown in Fig. 145. The joists are laid on the cellar or foundation walls, for the first floor, then a rougn floor may be laid on these joists, and the string pieces for the partitions may be laid on this floor, or the partition studs may rest on the joists, good solid provision being made for this purpose.

Before the partitions are built in, the outside walls must be put up and properly plumbed and braced. These walls must rest on sills formed on the lines of some one of schemes or sections shown in the preceding pages. A section of one side of the house showing the bare walls is produced at Fig. 144. This figure shows the openings for windows, also ends of porch and kitchen, with two sections of roof on different levels. The lines of joists on the second floor are shown in Fig. 145, also the direction of rafters, ridges and hips in the various roofs. While the house under discussion is a small one, the methods of erection are those that may be applied to the building of all kinds of balloon structures, large or small.

A building of greater pretensions is shown at Fig. 146. The windows and doors show double studding all round. This is always a good plan to adopt, but necessarily uses up quite a lot more material than is actually required; 2x4 blocks nailed on the studs here and there, would answer quite well to nail the finish to, but if a building be boarded on both sides of the wall, neither blocks nor a second stud would be necessary. One objectionable feature in this frame is the use of 2x8 inch joists in the attic floor. These joists are too light for the space they run over; they should at least be 2x10-inch, then there would be little danger of the floor sagging, particularly if the floor joists were well bridged.

Dormers should be framed as shown in the section drawing, Fig. 147. An opening of the proper size to receive the dormer should be framed in the roof, and the studs of the dormer should be notched out one inch over the roof boarding and trimmer rafter and extended to the floor. Notching the studding onto the roof prevents the roof from sagging or breaking away from the sides of the dormer and thus causing a leak, and the studding being extended to the floor also stiffens the trimmer and gives a homogeneous surface to lath on, without fear of plaster cracks. An enlarged section through the dormer sill is also given in Fig. 147 showing the way in which the flashing should be placed. The flashing should be laid over the second shingle and the third shingle laid

over it. This keeps the flashing in place and looks better. The upper edge of the flashing should be securely nailed to the back of the sill. As soon as the walls of a frame building are up they should be covered with hemlock, spruce or pine boards, dressed one side and free from shakes and large knot holes. When the brace frame is used it is generally customary to sheath the first story before the second story studding is set up. The sheathing or boarding should be nailed at each bearing with two tenpenny nails, although eight-penny nails are often used. If the building is built with a balloon frame it is necessary to put the boarding on diagonally in order to secure sufficient rigidity in the frame. With the braced frame diagonal sheathing is not necessary, although it makes a better job than when laid horizontally, and all towers, cupolas, etc., should be sheathed in this way.

In covering the roof two different methods are pursued, in the first the roof is tightly covered with dressed boarding, like the walls, and in the second narrow boards are nailed to the rafters horizontally and with a space of two or three inches between them. The latter method is considered to make the more durable roof, as it affords ventilation to the shingles and causes them to last longer. But if the attic is to be finished such a roof is very hot in summer and cold in winter, and most architects prefer to cover the roof with boarding laid close together and then lay tarred paper over the boarding and under the shingles or slate; this not only better protects the attic space from changes in temperature, but also prevents fine snow from sifting in under the slate or shingles. The specifications should distinctly mention whether the boards are to be laid close together or laid open, as well as the kind and quality of the boards.

Tinned roofs should be covered with matched boards, dressed one side, and all holes covered with sheet iron, and the ridges planed off. Figs. 148 and 149 show how a village church spire may be constructed by the use of scantlings 2x6 and 2x8 inches. The corner posts

are formed of three pieces 2x6 inches spiked together. The other heavy parts are formed in like manner. Plans of the structure are shown at A and B. Of course this style of structure can be changed and adapted to suit almost any style of spire or tower; but it is not my intention to give many examples of spires, roofs, towers or steeples in this part, as I intend to show a number of such in Part 2 of this volume. I will, however, add a few light timbered examples, as they may be considered as balloon framing.

In the formation and construction of an ogee roof, many things are to be considered, and as many of these roofs are built up of light timbers and covered with thin and flexible materials it will not be considered out of place to notice a few examples at this point. Fig. A 150 shows a quarter plan A B of the timbers of an ogee roof to a circular tower. The three purlins also shown in the plan are marked 1, 2, 3, in the elevation. The division for the boarding on the outside is indicated by C D, that for the inside boards being indicated by G H, while intermediate bearers for additional fixing for boarding are numbered 4 to 8 in the elevation. Some of these bearers may be omitted at discretion. Fig. B 150 shows elevation and vertical sections of the wall plate, which is formed of two pieces, each 2 in. thick by 4 in. wide, with, joints crossed, and having crossed bearers out of 6 in. by 4 in. stuff, halved together at the center and at the plate; all being flush both sides and securely bolted to the plate with 4 in. by ⅝ in. bolts. The center post is out of 6 in. by 6 in. octagonal stuff, is stump-tenoned into the bearer at the foot, and secured with 1 in. bolts. This post may at option be carried up above the cap, and finished with ornamental turned or octagonal worked finial. The ogee rafters are 4½ in. wide and are made up of two in. thicknesses. The joints are crossed and securely fixed together with screws or clenched nails, are stump tenoned into the plate at the bottom, and are shouldered into the post at the top, as shown by the solid line, and stump tenoned as shown by dotted lines (see section Fig.

B).

The rafters are secured to the plate at the foot with angle irons 6 in. or 8 in. long by *2y2* in. or 3 in. wide and 14 in. or % in. thick, fixed with % in. coach screws or bolts. Purlins 1 to 3 are the main purlins. Additional purlins 4 to 8 may be introduced if necessary. Dotted lines carried down from section to plan show the length required, and the section Fig. 155 shows the size of stuff required for cutting. Fig. 151 shows the main purlins (1 to 3) for one-quarter; the sections, and the surplus stuff to be cut away, being shown by black shading. These purlins can be cut out of 4 in. by 9 in. deals, and with very little waste of material if the inside (commonly called the belly) is cut out first and glued on the back edge, two ribs being thus *1* got out of each 9 in. deal.

Fig. 152 shows the intermediate purlins or bearers for one-eighth of the circle. Moulds are taken from the plan in the same way as for the main purlins, and the bevels for squaring are obtained in the same way in each case. Fig. 153 shows (looking upwards) the turned cap, perforated to allow of sliding on to the octagonal post. The shape of the outer thickness of the cover boarding is shown by Fig. 154. The method of obtaining the mould for these boards is as follows: First, divide the quarter C to D into the same number of spaces as the predetermined number of boards to be used. Next, divide, on the outside, the line of covering into say twelve equal spaces—the more spaces the greater the accuracy (see section numbered 0 to 12). Lay out these spaces in a straight line (see Fig. 154) to get the stretchout of the ogee from the back of the ogee (see the dotted lines on the plan), carry down a line to the center of one of the boards on the quarter (see X X). Take in the compasses the width of the board each way from the center, and transfer these widths on the stretch-out line as Fig. 154. Trace the widths from point to point, and the necessary mould will be complete. Let the mould be of the full given width. To allow for the slight difference made by the curve of the board, the joints will be slightly wreathed. This wreathing may be accurately obtained by following for the lower thickness the same instructions given for the upper, when the difference in the widths of the two boards will give the wreathing necessary. The boards, for convenience of bending, may consist of two thicknesses of % in. of 7/16 in. stuff; if % in. that thickness has been specified. In fixing, let them lap over the joints by allowing the center line of the lower board to be the joint line of the upper board. Fig. 155 shows the inner edge of the rafters, with their joints and tenons. Circular towers in framed construction may be divided into two classes, namely, those which have their foundations on a line connected with the main foundation of the house, and second those which are carried up from the second floor, resting on, or being supported by, the floor beams of the second story. The latter class will be considered, as it embodies more important construction, although some of the matters which will be treated are applicable to all circular towers. The first thing for the practical carpenter or builder to consider is how to so construct the floor as to support the tower in a proper manner; that is, so that it will sustain with perfect safety the weight to be placed upon it.

Referring to Fig. 156, which is supposed to represent the general appearance of a tower built on an angle to a house. It is placed at the right hand of the front of the building, and is designed to form an alcove closet, or an extension to the corner room. Its plan, as may be seen in Fig. 158, is a three-quarter circle, the apex of the angle at the corner being the center from which the circular plan is struck. The radius of the plate outside is three feet nine inches thus making the tower 7 feet 6 inches in diameter. It is intended that the tower floor shall be level with a room in the second story and the beams or joists must be framed in such a manner that the flooring can be laid in the circle of the tower, while at the same time being so secured as to support the weight of it. The form of construction indicated in Fig. 158 of the engravings is well adapted for the purpose, and an inspection will show that it consists of a double header made of 2x10 inch timbers placed diagonally across the corner at a sufficient distance back from it to give ample leverage to counterbalance the weight suspended outside the plate. The tower beams are framed square into this header on the outside and the floor beams are framed into it on the inside. By this construction a cantilever is formed, for the header in carrying the main beams forms a counterpoise for the superadded weight, which is borne by the unsupported beams which project outside. It will be readily seen that this, obviously, is a good construction, and much better than introducing many short timbers after the manner indicated in Fig. 159. In the latter case the leverage outside being much greater than that inside, the plate being the fulcrum, there is a strong probability of its tearing away from the main framing. For the same reason it is regarded as a serious mistake to attempt to radiate the timbers as indicated by the dotted lines in Fig. 159. The position of the timbers are shown in the elevation of the framing, Fig. 157, and we have no doubt that practical builders will fully appreciate what has been pointed out.

When the beams are inserted and the main framing has been nailed, a bottom circular plate, or template, marked A, in Fig. 157, is made from two thicknesses of 1 inch stuff, and nailed on exactly the size required. The position of the window studs is also marked on it, as represented in Fig. 158. The upper plate, or which is really the wall plate proper, and indicated hy B in Fig. 157 of the engravings, must also be made, and this will rest on the top ends of the studding and support the rafters. This plate will be a complete circle measuring 7 feet 6 inches in diameter and struck with a 3 foot 9 inch radius rod and laid out upon the floor, as indicated in the roof framing plan, Fig. 160. The pieces necessary to form the upper and lower plates may be sawn out of rough 1 inch pine boards from one pattern, which may be any one of those drawn in the plan, and a number of which go to make up the whole plate. The studding are cut 11 feet 8 inches, which being added to 4 inches, the thickness of the plates, makes the entire height 12 feet. The window headers, both at the top and bottom are likewise circular and are framed in after the manner represented in Fig. 157 to form the openings and cripple or short studding cut in under them in the center. All studding must be set perfectly plumb and all plates and headers perfectly level. In order to insure this it is well to be certain that.the bottom plate is level by placing a parallel straight edge with a spirit level on top of it, across the plate at different points. Then, if the studding be cut in equal length the upper plate must, in consequence, be placed in a level position. A number of horizontal sweeps, 2 inches thick and 4 inches wide, as indicated at C, in Fig. 157, require to be cut out to form ribbing or pieces nailed in 16 inches apart, to which the vertical boarding outside and the lath and plaster inside are fastened. It will be seen that if this construction is followed the whole cylindrical wall can be very strongly and economically built up. To save time and labor and also to expedite matters, the sweeps may be sawed out at the mill with a band saw, although it can be done in pine with the compass saw.

With regard to the molded roof, it may be said that having a molded outline it will necessarily require molded rafters sawn to the curvature called for in the elevation. As a general thing, architects furnish a full size working detail for roofs of this kind, but it often happens that it is not forthcoming and the carpenter or builder is obliged to strike out a pattern rafter himself. To do this quickly and as accurately as possible, it is well to lay out the whole roof on a floor, something after. the following manner: Referring to Fig. 161, draw any base line 7 feet 6 inches in length, as A B, and divide exactly in the center, or at 3 feet 9 inches, as C. From C square up the line to 9 feet high, as C D, and divide this line into 13 equal divisions, as 1, 2, 3, 4, 5, 6 etc. Through these points draw lines parallel to A B or square C D any length on each side of C D. Now, from the point D dress

the curve of the rafter, as indicated by the letters E, F, G, H, I, J, K, L, M, N, 0 and P, as near to the outline as possible. A very good method of obtaining these curves is to divide the architect's 4 inch scale drawing by horizontal division lines similar to those in Fig. 161, and to scale off the lengths from the axis or vertical line C D. By setting off these measurements on a full size lay out, points will be obtained through which the flexure of the curves may be very accurately determined.

The 16 rafters may all be drawn from the one pattern, as they are all alike and should be framed to fit against a 3 inch wood (boss), as indicated by X in Fig. 160, in order to obtain a solid nailing at the peak. In this engraving rafters are shown in position in elevation and also in plan, as well as the way they radiate or are spaced around the circle 16 inches apart on the plate. As it is always best to board such roofs as this vertically, ribbing or horizontal sweeps will have to be cut in between the rafters, and as there should be as many of these as possible for the purpose of giving a strong framework to hold the covering boards, it is advisable to cut in one at each of the divisions marked on the elevation shown in Fig. 161. The outline plan of this figure represents the top lines of these sweeps, which are well nailed in between the rafters. Fig. 162 of the engravings shows the exact size of the headers and their positions when nailed in. They are struck from different radii, which shorten as they go upward. It will be noticed that each set of sweeps is consecutively numbered with the lines C 1, 2, 3, etc., from C to D of Fig. 161. There will be 15 sweeps in each course and, therefore, 15 different patterns. They may be conveniently numbered and marked in the following manner: For No. 2, for example, a pattern can be cut and marked "Pattern for 15 sweeps, No. 2." There will, therefore, be 180 altogether to be cut out, and these should be cut 116 a trifle longer than the exact size, in order to allow for fitting.

At Figs. 163 to 166, I show the construction of a domical roof with a circular opening in the center for a sky-

light. Two of the main principals, C D and the corresponding one, are framed with a king-post c, as shown in Fig. 165; the others at right angles to these, with queen-posts, as seen in Fig. 166. The main ribs correspond to the principals, and the shorter ribs are framed against curbs between them, as at a Figs. 163 and 165.

Figs. 167 and 168 show the framing of an ogee domical roof on an octagonal plan. The construction will be readily understood by inspection; and the method of finding the arris ribs, shown in Fig. 169 will be understood from what may be said when treating of hip-rafters.

Figs. 170, 171, 172 and 173 show the construction of a domical roof with a central post b, Fig. 172, into the head of which four pairs of trussed rafters are tenoned; four intermediate trusses Fig. 173, are framed into the same post at a lower level. The collars are in two flitches as shown at c Fig. 172, and are placed at different heights so as to pass each other in the middle of the span. The collars of two trusses at right angles to each other may be on the same level, and halved together at their intersection, as shown at Fig. 173. The curved ribs are supported by struts from the principals, as seen in Figs. 172 and 173. The plan and elevation Figs. 170 and 171 exhibit the curved arrises which the sides of the horizontal ribs assume when cut to the curvature of the dome, as at a Fig. 172.

In connection with these domical or curved roofs it may not be amiss to give a few examples of the methods by which the various curves are obtained for the hips and cripples or jack rafters, that are to cut in against the hip. Generally, the major or regular rafter, will be cut on an irregular curve, or elliptical as will be seen at Fig. 174 this sketch, the dotted curved line from A to g represents one method, while the curved line between the two points following the intersections of lines at A 6 c d e and / with horizontal lines H I J K and T, must be the exact position for the major rafter at each of these points. More points may be taken in the same manner, according to the requirements of the case. The major rafter can be taken in this manner from any shape that it may be desirable to employ in the minor rafters.

Another example is shown at Fig. 175. Here the common or major rafter is laid down first, then mark the seat of the hip rafter and draw in the ordinates, as shown by the dotted lines, and employ as many as seems desirable, the number being immaterial. Extend them downward until they cut the seat of the hip rafter. Square out from the seat, and make the different heights measured from it correspond with the lines from which they are derived. Then take a thin batton strip and bend it to suit the points thus established. Mark in around the batton. This will give the true shape of the hip rafter. Now lay off half the thickness of the hip rafter, parallel with the seat as shown, and where the ordinates cut it, square out, as shown by the dotted lines. Also square out with the ordinates in the hip. Draw in the short lines cutting the sweep and the dotted ordinates. This gives the required backing, as may be seen by the dotted sweep. In the third place, to more thoroughly understand why all this should be, take a piece of large cove molding as shown in Fig, 176, then cut one end square and one end a miter and square down the ordinate as seen on the square sections. Carry the lines along the bottom of the piece, and square them again across the miter section. When this has been done, let him see if it will fit a true circle. Let me here remark that when any circular body is cut on an angle the section ceases to be round and becomes elliptical. This is a fact well worth keeping in mind. There are many other methods of obtaining curves for this kind of work, and when I come to discussing heavy timber framing and roofing, I may take the subject up again.

In the framing of mansard and curb roofs with light scantlings, many methods are in vogue, some very good, some otherwise. I will have more to say on this subject, too, later on. The method I show here at Fig. 177 should commend itself to all good f ranters, as being neat,

strong and economic. It is built up with small timbers and is quite sufficient.

The two schemes for mansard roofs shown at Fig. 178, are in a measure self-explanatory. They are formed with light scantlings and joists, the sizes of timbers being given on sketches. The joists of the attic floor serve as the main ties, and are spiked to the wall-plates. In No. 1 the common rafters forming the lower slopes of the roof are nailed to the joists, and supported in the middle by studding. They are cut out at the top in bird'smouth form to support the continuous plate, on which the upper rafters and ceiling joists rest. A more elaborate arrangement is shown in No. 2, where the lower slopes of the roof are curved, and an eaves cornice of wide projection is constructed. A partition is introduced at A, so that the walls of the rooms are vertical. For roofs of ordinary buildings, cottages, dwellings or even country villas the examples shown will be quite strong enough to do all service required of them. For larger and more extensive buildings, heavier and larger timbers will be required, and under the head of Heavy Timber Roofs in the second part of this volume, I will deal with mansard and other roofs at length.

For a light trussed roof, that is self-supporting, the German Truss, so called, for light stiff work, is an excellent arrangement. Fig. 179, shows the method of construction and Fig. 180, some details of same. This truss is generally known as the scissor-beam truss. Here the collar-beam is in compression, and the parts or timbers mostly being double as shown in details C and B. The rafters being supported in the middle are more than twice as strong as in a couple-close roof of the same span. The ends of the collars may be halved on to the rafters and secured with nails or bolts. A board may be clinch-nailed to unite the three pieces at the apex. Trussed-rafter roofs of this and other kinds involving a considerable amount of labor may, for the sake of economy, be spaced farther apart then ordinary rafters, stronger slats being used for the slating, and furring strips being fixed to receive the plasterer's laths.

Another roof, somewhat similar to the one just shown, is exhibited at Fig. 181. This is more eco nomical than the previous example so far as labor is concerned, but is by no means as good or efficient, but will be found quite efficient where the span is not more than 30 feet; where the timbers cross each other they must be either well spiked together, or have carriage bolts put through them and well tightened. It often occurs that the carpenter is called upon to build a ventilator or belfry on a stable or other building and in order to meet this emergency I submit the sketches Figs. 182 and 183, which I think will often prove useful. We suppose the roof to be already constructed and the upper work, as shown at 182, built over the ridge with very light timbers; Fig. 183 shows the ventilator and a portion of the stable in a finished condition.

Many bay windows are now built without having a foundation from the ground, the whole being projected from the wall of the building and a few hints and suggestions as to the construction of a window of this kind may not be out of place at this point.

In Fig. 184, is shown a detail of the manner in which the sills and joists in a house are built. The foundation wall is of cement, the sill of 2x8 inch material. The joists are 2x10 inch material placed sixteen inches on centers. On the plan where the bay-window comes the joists should be longer and should be extended past the wall eighteen inches, as shown in detail, Fig. 185. These joists support the bay. As a rule a templet is made from plan and is used to lay out window on joists and they are cut to conform with it. It is customary to spike on the ends of the joists pieces of the same material to strengthen the work. I have found that by using studs 2x4 inches as plates and spiking them on top of the joists, as shown in Fig. 185, was all that was necessary to make a good strong job. After plates have been nailed on the joists they are cut plumb down from the outside edge of plate, so that the sheathing may be nailed on. Care must be taken to have the plates true with plan. The studding being erected in the main building, put up the studding in the bay window. There should be two at each angle or a solid piece may be got out to place here. The other studding should be placed sixteen inches on center. Double plates are used and stay lathed true with templet. The roof plan is shown in Fig. 186. The roof has a raise of one foot above the plate. Rafters are framed and put on as in detail Fig. 186. Then they are cut off on plumb eleven inches Irom sheathing. Lookouts are nailed on rafters and toenailed in sheathing, care being taken to have them all the same distance from the top of plate and true. The material for lookouts may be 1x6 inches framed as in Fig. 187. The planceer board is fitted and nailed on lookouts, facia boards fitted and put on, also crown moulding, the top of which should be even with top of roof boards. Shingles being used the hips should be flashed with galvanized iron, also flashing put on against sheathing on house. The window is sheathed np and the window frames set true. Then we can put on the watertable. Friese boards are put on and the bed mould, which finishes between friese and planceer boards, as in Fig. 187. Sometimes corner boards are used on angles. Of course they make the work easier, but a better looking job can be done by mitering the clapboards on these angles. Often a small strip of inch and one-eighth material is fitted to use in the angles against main building. This gives good results as the main part or bay can be clapboarded separately as well. We would advise that a miter-box be made and used to cut clapboards at angles, and if care is taken in laying it out and in the way the siding is put on it to expedite the work. A story-rod should be used to lay off for siding. We have often seen many jobs where poor workmanship and slack methods were used, also on some jobs where three or four more clapboards were used on one side than on the other, illustrating the need of a story-rod. At Fig. 188 is shown the skeleton framework complete ready to receive whatever covering may be decided upon. The window frames will, of course, be made to fill

the openings and should be put in place after the frame is rough boarded and papered. Good paper should be well wrapped around the window studs in order to exclude wind, and if the work is properly done, the whole can be made as warm and as airtight as any other part of the house.

In many localities long scantlings are hard to get and are very costly. To overcome this, 2x4 inch scantlings may be spliced by putting the ends together and nailing pieces of inch stuff on each side of the joint from 18 to 24 inches long and this will make a strong splice for studs that stand on end. Of course, if the stud happens to be for a corner or for a door, or a window jamb, the splicing piece must not show inside the opening as it would interfere with the window or door frame. Sometimes studs are lengthened by allowing them to lap over each other and the lap spiked together with four inch spikes or nails. This is not a good method and should only be made one use of in certain conditions when little or no weight is to rest on the studs. A stout piece of scantling of the same section as the studding, may be nailed or spiked along the end joints, making a splice that does its work very well.

In putting up a balloon frame with short studs it is usual to put it up in single stories. The first story should be completed as far as the framing is concerned and a rough floor laid for the second story, on this floor 2x4 inch stringers should be laid all around the building on a line with the outside walls and the window and other openings should be marked off on these stringers, and where possible this upper studding should stand direct over the studding in the lower story; and if this occurs between the joists of the second floor short pieces of studding should be "cut" in between the plate of' the first story and the stringer and nailed in solid, which will throw the weight of the upper studding onto the lower studs. Buildings erected this way are strong enough to resist all ordinary wind pressures, but in all cases it is best to board up the outside of the frames diagonally. This insures the

tying of the stories together, making the whole building very much stronger and rendering it so that the wind would have to be strong enough to blow over the whole building before the upper portion would budge.

Before leaving balloon or light framing, it will not be amiss to show a few examples of eave or cornice framing suitable to both light or heavy timber work. Fourteen examples are exhibited from Figs. 189 to 203 inclusive. Fig. 189' shows a very plain cornice with the rafter cut so as to partly rest on the plate, with a portion running over the plate to form the projection and eave. The method of finishing is also shown. Fig. 190 exhibits a somewhat more elaborate cornice with gutter trough at B. In this case the planceer stands out at right angles from the wall.

Fig. 191 shows a rafter projecting out and over the wall about three and a half feet and dressed and moulded. It will be seen that the projection is of different pitch to the main roof, and this necessitates the projecting and being a separate piece with the inside end spiked to the main rafter as shown.

Fig. 192 shows a cornice where the projecting ends of the ceiling joists play an important part in the construction of the work. The rafter rests on the ceiling joists and is notched over the plate, which may be notched into the joists or spiked in them as shown. The ends of the joists are trimmed off to slope of roof.

Fig. 193 also shows projecting ceiling joists with ends of rafters spiked to joists. This is not good construction but may be used where the roof is not extensive.

Fig. 194 shows an old time cornice with a wooden gutter. This style is seldom used riow-adays, but sometimes people living in the country insist on employing it.

Fig. 196 exhibits another cornice on nearly the same lines as Fig. 194. I may say here, that instead of wooden gutters, heavy galvanized sheet iron gutters could be employed to advantage.

Fig. 197 shows a rafter resting in a foot mortise or crow-foot in a solid heavy timber frame. This style of framing rafters is often used in heavy timber work, such as barns, stables, warehouses, freight sheds and similar structures.

Fig. 198 shows another cornice which is intended to have a wooden gutter. The method of finishing the rafter on the lower end to receive the gutter is shown.

Fig. 199 shows a cornice designed for a brick or stone house having a curve at the eave. The method of finishing is shown and is quite simple, the furring being the main thing in forming the curve for the bed of the shingles or slate.

Fig. 200 shows a very good method of forming a cornice for a balloon frame. It is very simple, easily formed and quite effective.

Fig. 201 shows a cornice where the pitch of the roof suddenly changes at the projection, as is sometimes the case with towers, balconies and over hay windows. The method of construction is shown very clearly in the illustration and may readily be followed.

Fig. 202 shows an ornamental cornice which may be used either on cottage or veranda work. A portion of the rafters shows as brackets below the planceer.

Fig. 203 shows a part of a veranda roof, with brackets, gutter, and facia. Here the roof has a very low pitch and the rafters are nailed against the sides of the ceiling joists and the depression for the gutter is cut out at the end of the rafter as shown. The gutter, of course, like all similar gutters, is lined with galvanized iron, zinc or tin.

These examples of cornices are quite sufficient for the framer to have by him; if other designs are required, the workman should experience no difficulty in forming what he wants, having these designs at his command.

INTRODUCTION TO PART II. *"Heavy Timber Framing"* is an art that requires considerable skill on behalf of the man who "lays out" the work, because of the fact that this work must be carried on without "trying" how the work coincides, or in other words, without being able to make use of the good old-fashioned rule of '' cut and fit.'' The lengths, cuts, locations and duties of each piece of timber used in the construction of heavy frame work, must be considered by the framer, and each piece entering into the building, must be mortised and wrought separately. This is no easy task, and the person undertaking it assumes no small responsibility and his position is such as should insure to him a remuneration commensurate with the position and responsibility he accepts. Unfortunately, the "boss framer" receives as pay but very little more than the regular carpenter, something that is not as it should be, and if he were not ambitious, and proud of his ability as a framer, he would not accept the position, but rather take a place among the ordinary workmen and thus escape the responsibilities of "Bosship." 151 PART II. HEAVY TIMBER FRAMING.

"Is heavy timber framing a lost art?" This question has been asked me many times during the past twenty years and I have invariably answered it in the negative.

"Heavy timber framing is not a lost art." If necessity arose tomorrow in the United States or Canada, for the services of five thousand competent framers they would be forthcoming within a period of sixty days if inducements were *sufficiently* attractive. Since the introduction of steel frames into building construction, the use of timber frames in roofs, buildings, bridges and trestle work has greatly fallen off, particularly in or near large cities, where timber has become scarce and costly, but in the west, north, and south, timber structures are often made Use of, and will be for many decades yet. Indeed, even when steel is made use of timber has to be frequently employed in special cases; so that a knowledge of framing is as necessary to the general workman today as it ever was. When I say this, I do not mean that it is necessary to become an expert framer, but that a knowledge of the proper way to handle and 152 lay out timber, should be possessed by every man who aspires to be a competent carpenter.

Heavy framing is an art that requires considerable ability and intelligence on the part of the operator, inasmuch as it is not one of those branches of the trade where the "cut and fit" process can be applied. Each piece of timber, whether it be a girt, a chord or beam, a post, brace, sill, girder, strut or stringer, must be dealt with, and given its proper shape, length and relationship to the part or parts it is to be connected with, without its being brought in direct contact with it until all is ready to be put together and pinned up solid. A clear head and a good memory, along with the faculty of exactness, are absolutely necessary qualifications for the making of a good framer. He must see to it that all tenons are the right size to suit the mortises which they are intended to fill, and that all mortises are clearly and smoothly finished and not too large or too small to snugly receive the tenons, and all this must be done without any "trying and fitting." The charm of good framing lies in the fact that every mortise and tenon must be '' driven home'' with a heavy wooden mall; but tenons should not fit so tight as to require more than ordinary driving.

The tools required by the heavy timber framer are not numerous, but are heavy and somewhat costly. I give a list of most of the tools employed herewith:

An ordinary chopping axe.,

A good heavy headed adze.

A heavy 8 or 10 inch blade broadaxe.

A carpenter's 4 or 5 inch hatchet.

A ten foot pole made of hardwood.

A steel square, ordinary size.

A bridge builder's square with 3 inch blade.

Two or three good scratch awls.

Chalk lines, spools and chalks.

Several carpenter's heavy lead pencils.

One or two pairs of "winding sticks" or battons.

One "slick" or slice with $Sy2$ or 4 inch blade.

A good jack plane and a smoothing plane.

A boring machine with four augers.

Three or four assorted augers for draw-boring

An ordinary sized steel crow-bar.

An adjustable cant-hook, medium size.

A couple of good hickory or ironwood handspikes.

A half dozen 4 inch maple rollers. Four good framing chisels, 2 in., iy2 in. , 14 in., and 1 in.

A two-hand cross-cut saw about 5 feet long. A good hand-saw, also a good rip-saw. Two oil stones, and a good water-of-Ayr-stone. Sometimes a medium weight logging chain will be found very useful.

An adjustable bevel will come in handy at times.

These, with a few other tools that will suggest themselves from time to time as the work progresses, will he all that will be necessary to frame the most complicated frame structure.

While I do not intend to give a lengthy description of these tools or give prosy directions. regarding their use, care and management, I deem it proper to say a few words on the subject: The common chopping or woodman axe is so well known to every American that I need not say much of it at this juncture. It is one of the most useful tools the framer possesses, as it can be used for so many purposes; indeed, in the hands of some workmen it can be made to take the place of several tools. It is sharpened from both faces.

The next in order will be the adze, which should have a good heavy steel faced pole or head. This should have a well tempered cutting blade not less than three inches wide, and should have a handle shaped as shown in Fig. 204. This is a dangerous tool for the inexperienced workman to use, and differs from the SLX'e, EL'S the cutting edge is at right angles with the handle. It has been named "The Devil's shin hoe," as it has made many a serious wound in workmen's shins. It is ground from one face only. At Fig. 205 I show the style of chisel that should be used in framing. These can be obtained in any sizes from half inch to three inches. They are heavy and strong and with care will last a lifetime.

The hatchet shown at Fig. 206 is a very handy tool for the framer, and may be used for many purposes, more particularly for making pins or pegs to fit the draw-bores. It is also useful for splitting off the surplus wood from the shoulders of the tenons.

The mallet shown at Fig. 207 is a common type and is used for beating mortises or hammering the chisels. These mallets are made in several forms, some with square heads like the one shown, or with round heads, Fig. 207l/o, having flat faces, and are often protected on their working faces by leather, and having iron hoops driven on them to protect the working faces from splintering or battering when being used on the chisel.

The boring machine, shown at Fig. 208, is used for relieving the mortises of their cores and making them easier to "beat" out with the chisel and mallet. This machine can be adjusted for angle boring as well as vertical. A loose auger is also shown. Generally four augers of various sizes are sold with each machine.

Hand saws will be found very useful, the crosscut, as shown at Fig. 209, for cutting the shoulders, and the rip-saw for cutting the tenons, and uses for both will be found in much other work about a frame building besides shoulders and tenons.

Fig. 207M.

The long cross-cut saw is an indispensable tool to the framer (Fig. 210) for cutting off timber, cutting shoulders and other work. It is scarcely necessary to show illustrations of the other tools required by the framer, as we may have occasion to refer nn l illustrate them later on.

Thirty years ago it was the custom in most of the States where there was standing timber for the framer to go into the woods, choose the timber for his work, fell it, rough hew it, and finally have it hauled to the location, by oxen or horses, to where the barn, house, or bridge was to be erected. This practice, I am informed, is still continued in Maine and several of the Western States, but owing to the fact that saw-mills are so. numerous in wooded districts, capable of cut ting timber to any reasonable

length, the practice of hewing has fallen almost into disuse; and because of this fact I deem it inexpedient to show and describe the various methods of manufacturing square timber from the round.

It is often necessary to mortise and tenon round logs for rough work, and to enable the young workman to accomplish this I show, at Fig. 211, a simple method of finding the lines for this kind of work. The illustration shows a round stick of timber, with chalk lines oo and RE struck on two sides of it. These lines are first laid out on the pattern x, as shown, from which they are transferred to some point on the timber, as nearly the center of its cross section as possible at each end of the stick and as plumb from the center as can be obtained. The pattern x which is formed of two boards—any reasonable length—nailed together exactly at right angles to each other, with the ends cut off square, must then have a line drawn on both its faces, as shown at P P. The pattern is then laid on the timber, the top line being made to correspond with the lower line on the pattern. From this lower line, the second chalk line on the side of the timber should be struck. The end of the pattern forms a square, and if the timber is cut off on the lines of the end of the pattern, that end will be at right angles with the axis of the timber.

Mortises and tenons may be laid off from the chalk lines by measurements as may readily be seen. Lines drawn across the mortises by aid of the pattern will be at right angles to their sides; the tenons may be laid off in the same manner, and by correct measurement made so as to fit into the mortises snug and tight. If it is desirable to "draw-bore" this work, it may be done by a proper use of the pattern by pinking a hole through it where the draw pin is to pass through the mortise and tenon. If a square bearing is required for the shoulders at the tenons, it may be readily done by squaring across the mortise, using the pattern for the purpose.

This, perhaps, is all the information on the subject of round timbers the ordinary workman will ever require, but should he require more he should have no trouble in getting through with his work, as the foregoing contains the whole principle of working round timber. First, the board pattern as described, then line up the timber with straight chalk lines, and the whole system is opened up, so that any wideawake workman can manage the rest.

In working square timber, it is always necessary to have all points of junction square and "out of wind," or out of "twist" as some workmen call it. To take timber out of wind is quite a simple process—when you know how—and to "know, how" is a matter only of a few moments' thought and experience. The tools required to do this depend very much on the amount of "wind" or "twist" the timber may have. If a large quantity has to be taken off, as shown at Fig. 212, it will require an ordinary chopping axe and a broad axe; the first to lightly score or chip, and the last to finish the work smoothly. Sometimes a jack plane is used to finish the timber nicely when good clean work is required. The winding sticks or "batts" are placed on the timber as shown at Fig. 213, which gives an idea of the amount of wood that must be removed before the timber will have a fair plane surface. The manner of using the "batts" or winding sticks is shown at Fig. 214, where by sighting across the tops of the sticks the amount of winding can be easily detected.

The winding "batts," which are parallel in width, are placed across the wood (see Fig. 213), I and has the effect of multiplying the error to the length of the sticks. For this reason it is as well to make the sticks 1 ft. 6 in. to 1 ft. 8 in. long. To insure accuracy in long pieces of wood, the winding "batts" should be moved to two or three different positions down the length of the wood and the straight-edge used lengthwise.

It is not necessary to use the winding "batts" on either of the other surfaces of the wood, as the face edge is made at right angles to the face side, bringing into use the try-square and straight-edge. The other two surfaces are planed true to the gauge lines, which are put on par-allel to the first two surfaces. The writer has two of these winding "laths" which he made for himself over fifty years ago; they were made for bridge work and are made of black cherry, and are as true to-day *r 3* when they were first made.

In preparing timber for framing, it is not necessary that the whole timber be made to line, as this often entails a great deal of extra labor. The timber may be "spotted" or "plumbed" or "squared" at the points where girts, braces, studs or other timbers join the main timber. The object of this is to make a proper surface for the shoulders of tenons to sit against. This, however, may be very much assisted by adopting the following rules and making winding "batts" to suit the work.

J

The method, in full, may be described as follows: Referring to the illustrations, Fig. 215, shows what is called the wind batt. In taking the wind out of a timber, two wind batts are required. This wind batt consists of a piece of board *y2* by 4 in. and about 18 in. long. The edges of the batt must be made parallel to each other. Then a line is drawn down the center, leaving 2 inches" on each side of the line, as shown in the sketch. The brad awl is then stuck through the bot-tom half for the purpose of fastening to the end of the timber. The wind batts are then stuck on the ends of the piece of timber as shown in Fig. 217 of the sketches, half the batt projecting above the timber. The *19* operator then sights over the upper edges of the batts and moves either end until the edges coin-cide. He then takes the scratch awl and marks across the bottom edge of the batts at each end of the timber, as shown in Fig. 218. This completes one side. The rest is easy, as in the other side the wind is taken out by means of a steel square, as indicated in Fig. 217. Place the inside edge of the tongue of the square even with the line made by the wind batt, the outside edge of the blade being even with the smallest place on the outside of the

Fig. 217.

timber. Mark with a scratch awl down inside of the blade. Move the square up 2 inches on the timber and mark through to the top of the timber. The latter is then out of wind and the operator will proceed to line it, as shown in Fig. 216, which represents a stick of timber with the wind taken out and lined. Stick the scratch awl in the end of the timber at the point where the plumb lines cross each other, the awl being through the small loop in the line. All four sides of the timber may be lined without mov-ing the scratch awl. In taking the wind out of timber in this manner consider-able time is saved, as one man can take it out of wind and line it without other help.

From another source *(Carpentry and Building)* I get the following directions for preparing timber for framing from the pen of a practical framer who seems to know pretty well of what he is talking and starts off by saying: "The first step in the process is to scaffold your timber so that it will lie straight and as nearly level as possible, and so that you and your men who follow may work over it in a comfortable position. That done, suppose, as in Fig. 220, we have a cor-ner post to lay out which is 8% by 8% by 16 feet, and from shoulder to shoul-der of tenons is 15 feet. I would select the two best faces that give nearest a straight corner, taking a corner that is hollow rather than one that is full. Then I set one square on across the best face, far enough from the end for a tenon, and measure 15 feet towards the other end, making an irregular mark across the face at this point with a heavy pencil as I did at the other end. I then set my second square on this mark and look over the squares. Just here comes inthe nice point in unwinding timber. If at the first glance over the squares they should be very much in wind, then adjust the difference at each end by dividing. But this rule does not always work, for the wind may all be in the last two or three feet of the stick—more likely than not at the butt end. You will soon learn by looking over the faces of the timber to locate the cause or place of the wind. You will soon learn also that it requires but a slight change to adjust the squares so that there may be little cutting necessary in making the plumb spot. But to go on: With your adze or chisel (I mostly used a 3-inch slick) level off across the face of the timber as much as you think will be necessary to bring the lines right in the end. While at this end of the timber spot the side face, then go to the other end and unwind with the spot already completed. After making the plumb spot on the side face take your scratch awl and point with 2-in. face each way from your plumb spot, going around the four faces of the timber. Line through these points and work from the lines in laying out.

Suppose we have a cap sill to frame, full length, say 10 by 10 by 46 feet long and with the same bearings, bays each 14 feet and the floor 18 feet wide, all as represented by Fig. 221; I start at one end and measure through, making at the principal points (14 plus 18 plus 14 feet) with irregular pencil lines, selecting, of course, the best face for the outside. Then I test the timber through from end to end, looking over the squares before starting to unwind. If the squares line up well at first glance, then I go to work at one end and unwind through. If not then I try through at the other points. After deciding how and where to start, the process is similar to that of the post, and in like manner would I go about unwinding all the timbers of a frame.

From what I have just said you will observe that my rule for spotting timber was, at the shoulders of posts and at principal bearing of long timbers. Following this rule you will have true points where the most particular framing is to be done.

Sometimes, however, when I come to the short posts in the under frame, where several would be of the same length, including tenons, and a man at each end with square and pencil, as in Fig. 222, would unwind them, marking along the square across the end of post, allowing 2 in. for face. Square from this line on the same hand at each end with 2-inch face. Lining from these points we have the posts ready for laying out, as shown in Fig. 223.

Some framers think that time is saved by this method, hut I doubt it, for usually there is one side extra at each tenon to size, and I am inclined to advise that spotting in the manner first explained is the better way.

Fig. 224. Fig.

The two figures here given explain what I have just said about the extra sizing. Fig. 224 is the end of a post framed, where the plumb spot was made at the shoulder. Fig. 225 that of a post where the wind was taken out by the last process described, in which case, unless the timber was exceptionally well dressed, there was overwood and sizing as shown.

In ordinary framing it was not necessary to cut the plumb spot fully across the face of the timber—just far enough for the bearing to steady the square— 2 or 3 inches. If, however, you are required to do a very nice job of framing, and are paid for doing it, then cut your plumb spot fully across the face of the timber and choose the full instead of the hollow side for face. Line the overwood on both corners and counter hew. If the timber requires two faces, as for a post or wall plate, then turn the new face up, line and counter hew the other side. That done, mark your points, and line for laying out.

What do I use for lining? Chalk is good, but chalk washes off, and in the showery spring time, the barn builder's season, I generally used Venetian red and water in an old tin, the "boss" holding the tin and line reel with a crotched stick over the line, while one of the "boys" carried the line to the other end of the timber as it paid out. Under favorable circumstances, with one wetting, I was able to line the timber around on all sides.

There is one point worthy of notice, and in favor of the method of locating the plumb spot as given above: It serves as a check against mistakes in measurements. The process of laying out, as practiced by myself, was to unwind the timber as I have shown. Then starting at one end, scribe the extreme point and lay off the work there and work back again on the intermediate work. Coming

out right was almost proof that the work was correct, for, as you will readily see, the timber had then been measured three times."

These are excellent directions and are equally applicable to sawn as to hewn timbers. The workman will, now, I trust, be fully able to understand the importance of taking his timber out of wind, and the proper way to do it.

Fig. 226. I

The next thing to be considered are as what are known as "witness marks. " These marks are intended to inform the men who beat out the mortises, saw the tenons and clean up the gains and finish up the work generally after it has been set out by the boss framer. There are several methods of witnessing work by aid of the scratch awl which I show herewith, in Fig. 226; but, besides these, the work is sometimes witnessed with a pencil—blue, black or red; the black being used for mortises, the blue for tenons, and the red for gains or squared surfaces.

The end of the mortises and shoulders of tenons may be witnesses in the same manner, as shown in Fig. 226, using the pencil in lieu of scratch awL

In this diagram the letter Gr represents a gain, M is a mortise and T is a tenon, the short diagonal marks w in the upper piece being the witness marks. The sketch shows four different methods of witness marking which are employed by most workmen, while numerous combinations of these four methods are also often used.

The best of these witness marks are those used on the timber marked F, though ft has the dj advantage of being cut away when the mortise beaten or the tenon cut, so that should a blunder be made in the length of mortise or shoulder of tenon, it will be difficult to place the fault on the right person.

Another method of witnessing, and a very good one too, is shown in Fig. 227. T shows the tenon, M a mortise, A a gain, and H a halving. In this case it will be almost impossible to get astray if the workmen following the boss framer will only make himself acquainted with the system.

In Fig. 228 I show a method of witnessing a splice, and this, I think, will be readily understood. Another splice, with the manner of making it, is shown at Fig. 229, also the points where holes may be bored to receive bolts when such are to be bolted together for strength. The direction of the bolts is also shown. At Fig. 230 I show how to make witness mark to cut a shoulder on a brace. This brace shows two bevels, simply to indicate that no matter what the bevels may be the marks show the shoulders. The letter C is the shorter bevel. The lines A A marked off the sketch, Fig. 2C1, show how a line or seratch made by mistake may be marked so that it may be known as a line not to be used.

These witness marks are ample to instruct the workman in their uses, and though the examples given do not nearly cover the whole ground where such marks are required, they show the system and the keen workman will apply them in their proper places whenever it is necessary. i

Mortises and tenons are usually laid out with the steel square, but it is not the best or speediest way, though the square is always at hand and ready for use, and without a knowledge of its use for this purpose the workman will not be fully equipped for laying out a frame. Following an authority on the subject of laying out work by the steel square "the ends of the mortise are first struck as indicated at A and B, Fig. 232, and while the square is in the position indicated the mark C is made for the working side of the mortise, which is always the narrower side unless the two are equal. In practice it is best to mark the cut off at the end of the timber first, or if it does not need cutting off, place the square over the end of the stick, and mark back along the blade the *iy2,* 2 or 3 inches required for the shoulder. This makes sure that there is no projecting corners to give trouble later on.

If a tenon is being struck the same method is followed, going entirely around the stick but working in both directions from the face corner. The ends of the mortise or shoulder of the tenon

being thus treated, the sides are marked by reversing the square, placing the inside of the blade at E, Fig. 233, fair with the mark C previously made, and taking the same distance—in this case 2 inches— on the tongue of the square, as shown at B. Now by holding the square firmly with the thumb and fingers of the left hand both sides of the tenon can be marked, but great care is necessary to pre vent the 'slipping of the square. If there is any wane on the stick it is hard to tell when the mark D is exactly in line with the vertical face of the timber, and this matter must be determined by sighting down the side of the stick. It is also necessary to drop the blade of the square a little further, as at B, when squaring across a "wany stick."

In every heavy timber framing a bridge framing steel square could be employed. These have a blade three inches wide and a tongue one and a half inches wide. The blade is used to lay out mortises and tenons of three-inch dimensions. There is a slot one inch wide cut down the center of the blade, the slot is twenty-one inches long and it may be used on one inside edge to make a two-inch mortise or tenon; this is done by using one outside edge and one inside edge. These squares are made by Sargent & Co., of New York, and cost from $2.50 to $5.00 each. The squares are very handy for bridge builders and for framing all kinds of heavy timber.

A kind of templet or guide is made use of sometimes, for laying out work, it is much handier, and easier to work with than the square, and will aid in laying out work much more rapidly. These templets are made in both wood and metal. They are hinged at the angle as shown in the sketches herewith, so they may work easily over wany edges or can be folded together and stowed away in a tool chest.

Where there is much framing of a like character to do, it is always best to make a sheet iron templet, as the rubbing of the scratch awl against the working edges of a wooden brass bound one will wear away the surface and the tenons and mortises will not be the correct sizes.

Mr. Hobart, in *Carpentry and Building,* describes these templets—the wooden ones—and adds a fair description of them and the way to use them, and I reproduce in brief a portion of his article on the subject: '' The tool may be seen in two positions on the squared timber at Figs. 234 and 235. The tool is made of well seasoned wood % in. thick, three thicknesses being glued up to form a board 8 inches wide by 24 inches long. The boards are then mitred together lengthwise, as shown, and a pair of ornamental brass hinges put on, these being clearly indicated in the sketches. Each part of the board is then notched into four steps of 6 inches each, being made *iy2,* 3, 6 and 8 inches respectively. The other side of the tool is divided into 4, 6 and 8 inch steps, each 6 inches long. If much heavy work is to be laid out it will pay to make one side 1 inch wider, thus securing *iy2,* 3, 6 and 9 inch steps on that side. The notched edges of the board are finished with a great deal of exactness, and after cutting a little scant the edge is bound with a heavy strip of sheet brass, which is shaped and screwed to the marking edge. The marking edge, and the end as well, is marked off in inches and quarters, the same as a framing square,,and this proves a great convenience when using the tool.

In order to lay out a mortise, slide the tool along until the end comes flush with the longest corner; then mark the end of the mortise, as at E of Fig. 234. At the same time mark the other end of the mortise, F, Fig. 234; then slide back the marker and strike that line after having first struck the line E. Next reverse the tool and select the width of shoulder required—2 inches in this case— and mark alongside the board on the timber. This fixes one side of the mortise or tenon, and a mark alongside the right width of tool, H, Fig. 235, finishes that mortise in very quick time." Apart from this description, the workman will find in making use of this tool many places where it can be employed to advantage. If the whole tool was constructed of metal, it would not cost any more than if made of wood, as described in the foregoing, and it would be neater, lighter, much more compact, and would last for all time.

While it is true that this templet is a great help in rapid framing and while in some cases where the timber is wany or lacking on the arrises something of the kind is necessary. Where the writer has met with wany timber he has often tacked a planed board on the side of the timber to be worked keeping the upper edge even with the top of the timber, then the square can be used for making over as the board forms a good surface to work the square from. When the templet is used, the necessity of the board is done away with, as the vertical portion of it takes the place of the board. The method of using the square for cutting rafters, braces, and other angular work, has been shown and described elsewhere, so I drop the matter of the square for the present.

There is one matter in framing that I do not think has ever been described or properly illustrated, and that is the question of "boxing." Nonframer may not know what the term "boxing" means; but every "old hand" at the business has, no doubt, a vivid recollection of the term and its uses. "Boxing" in framing may be described as preparing a true real square with the jaws of the mortise for the shoulders of the tenon to butt solidly against. To accomplish this often requires the removal of portions of the timber before a flat square surface is found, and this may reduce the thickness of the tifriber operated upon. If we suppose four or five posts on the side of a building, and these posts are supposed to be 12 x 12 inches in section and in preparing these posts to receive the tenons it is necessary to remove over the face of each mortise one-quarter of an inch or more, and the girts or connecting timbers have their shoulders cut to suit the 12-inch posts, it will be seen that the length of the building at the line of girts will be less than intended. If forced into mortises made the proper distance apart in the sills, the outside posts will not Be plumb and it will be found impossible to make the plates fit in place, as the mortises on.the ends will

be found too far apart, and this would lead to all sorts of trouble and vexation. In boxing, we suppose the posts to be, say 11% inches instead of 12 inches. This allows half an inch for boxing, and this necessitates the girt between each set of posts, to be cut one inch longer between shoulders than if no boxing was prepared. In cases where posts are pierced on both faces and boxed, the post where the tenons enter, if directly opposite, may have to be reduced to 11 inches and must be accounted for on that basis. The young framer must be particular about the boxing and the necessary reduction of timbers when laying off his lengths of girts or bracing timbers, if not he will be sure to get into trouble or botch the job.

I show, at Fig. 236, how the boxing is done, and how to lengthen the timber between shoulders to meet the requirements of the case. Gr shows the girt where it is boxed into the post P, andt F S shows the sill and plate with the tenons T T relished for the shorter mortises. The brace B shows how it is butted at both ends against the boxing in the post and girt. The points, or '' toes,'' of the brace are squared off so as to rest against the half inch shoulder which is caused by the boxing.

At Fig. 237 I show a post boxed on both sides for braces; also a scarfing which ties two beams together, the joints of the beams being directly over the center of the post. It will be noticed the scarfing block grapples both beams and is bolted at both ends. The braces and post are draw-bored and pinned as shown by the round dots on the diagram. The scarfing block or bolster, in cases of this kind where there is a heavy weight above to carry, should be of hardwood, oak, maple or other suitable strong wood.

The next illustration, Fig. 238, shows a double boxed post with braces carrying a scarfed beam. The tenon on the top of the post passes through the splice holding the two beams together. It is drawbored and pinned together through both splices.

Fig. 239 exhibits another boxed post, braces, splice and beams. The post is

double pinned to both beams, which are bolted together. These two illustrations, Figs. 238 and 239, are good examples of spliced beam support, and are often made use of in warehouses, barns and other similar structures.

At Fig. 240 I show the usual manner of framing a barn about 30 x 40 feet, and 16 or 18 feet high. Fig. 241 exhibits a portion of the end of the building, with rafters, purlins and collar beam. The center post shown is supposed to be boxed on both sides, but the drawing is of too small a scale to show the boxing on either post, sill or plate.

The timbers for a building like this are usually about the following dimensions: Sills, 12 in. x 12 in.; posts and large girders, 10 in. x 10 in.; plates and girder over drive doors, 8 in. x 10 in.; purlin plates, 6 in. x 6 in.; purlin posts and small girders, 6 in. x 8 in.; braces, 4 in. x 4 in.; rafters, collar beams, etc. , 2 in. x 6 in. These dimensions may, of course, be changed to suit circumstances and conditions. All mortises in the heavy timber may be three inches and of such length as the sizes of the timber will allow. Draw-bore holes for pine may be from 1 in. to IV2 in. in diameter, but should never exceed the latter size. Two draw pins may be used in mortise and tenons when the tenon is 8 inches or more wide. Less than that width, one pin will be quite enough. In laying out draw-bore holes have them two inches from the side of the mortise, then on the tenons they should be an eighth or a quarter of an inch less than two inches from the shoulder, then if they are just two inches from the boxing or the face of the mortise, the pins, when driven in, will draw the shoulders snug up to the bearing. In making drawbore holes care must be taken not to make a mistake and place the hole where, when the pin is driven home, the joint will be forced open instead of drawn closer. A little thought when the holes are laid out will prevent the hole from being a *pushbore* instead of a draw-bore.

The braces are framed on a regular 3-foot run; that is, the brace mortise in the girder is 3 feet from the shoulder of the girder, and the brace mortise in the post is 3 feet below the girder mortise.

In this building the roof is designed to have a third pitch; that is, the peak of the roof would be one-third the width of the building higher than the top of the plates, provided the rafters were close-lyfitted ito the plates at their outer surfaces.

In order to give strength to the mortises for the upper end girders, these girders are framed into the corner post several inches below the shoulders of the post, say 4 inches; the thickness of the plates being 8 inches it will be perceived that the dotted line, AB, drawn from the outer and upper corner of one plate to the outer and upper corner of the other is just 1 ft. higher than the upper surface of the girder.

The purlin plates should always be placed under the middle of the rafters, and the purlin posts, being always framed square with the purlin plates, the bevel at the foot of these posts will always be the same as the upper end bevel of the rafters'; also, the bevel at each end of the gable-end girder will be the same, since the two girders being parallel, and the purlin post intersecting them, the length of the gable-end girder will be equal to half the width of the building, less 18 inches; 6 inches being allowed for half the thickness of the purlin posts, and 6 inches more at each end for bringing it down below the shoulders of the posts.

In order to obtain the proper length of the purlin posts, examine Fig. 241. Let the point P represent the middle point of the rafter, and let the dotted line PO be drawn square with AB; then will AC be the % of AB, or 7% feet, and PC, half » the rise of the roof, will be 5 feet, and PO 6 feet. The purlin post being square with the rafter, and PO being square with AB, we can assume that PR would be the rafter of another roof of the same pitch as this one, provided PO were half its width, and OR its rise. This demonstration determines also the place of the purlin post mortise in the girder; for AC being 7% feet, and OR being 4 feet, by adding these together, we find the point R, the middle of the mortise, to be 11%

feet from the outside of the building; and the length of the mortise being 71/ ± inches, the distance of the end of the mortise, next the center of the building, is 11 feet 9% inches from the outside of the building.

The brace of the purlin post must next be framed, and also the mortise for it, one in the purlin post and the other in the girder. The length of the brace and the lower end bevel of it will be the same as in a regular three feet run; and the upper end bevel would also be the same, provided the purlin post were to stand perpendicular to the girder; but, being square with the rafter, it departs further and further from a perpendicular, as the rafter approaches nearer and nearer towards a perpendicular; and the upper end bevel of the brace varies accordingly, approaching nearer and nearer to a right angle as the bevels at the foot of the post, or, what is the same thing, the upper end bevel of the rafter departs further and further from a right angle. Hence, the bevel at the top of this brace is a compound bevel, found by adding the lower end bevel of the brace to the upper end bevel of the rafter.

In framing the mortises for the purlin post braces, it is to be observed, also, that if the purlin , post was perpendicular to the girder, the mortises would each of them be 3 feet from the heel of the post; and the sharper the pitch of the roof, the greater this distance will be. Hence the true distance on the girder for the purlin post brace mortise is found by adding to 3 feet the rise of the roof in running 3 feet; which, in this pitch of 8 inches to the foot, is two feet more, making 5 feet, the true distance of the furthest end of the mortise from the heel of the purlin post.

The place in the purlin post for the mortise for the upper end of the brace may be found from the rafter table, by assuming that Ex would be the rafter of another roof of the same pitch as this one, if xy were half the width, and yE the rise. For then, since xy equals 3 feet, we should have width of building equal 6 feet, rise of rafter, one-third pitch, gives yE equal 2 feet; and hence xR would equal 3 feet 7.26 inches, the true

distance of the upper end of the mortise from the heel of the purlin post.

Figs. 242 and 243 are designed to illustrate the manner of finding the upper end bevel of purlin post braces, to which reference is made from the preceding examples.

In Fig. 242, let AB represent the extreme length of the brace from toe to toe, the bevel at the foot having been already cut at the proper angle of 45 degrees. Draw BC at the top of the brace, at the same bevel; then set a bevel square to the bevel of the upper end of the rafter, and add that bevel to BC by placing the handle of the square upon BC and drawing BD on the tongue. This is the bevel required.

Fig. 243 shows another method of obtaining the same bevel. Let the line AB represent the bevel at the foot of the brace, drawn at an angle of 45 degrees. Draw BD at right angles with AB, and draw BC perpendicular to AB, making two rightangled triangles. Then divide the base of the inner one of these triangles into 12 equal parts for the rise of the roof. Then place the bevel square upon the bevel AB at B and set it to the figure on the line CD, which corresponds with the pitch of the roof. This will set the square to the bevel required for the top of the brace. In this figure the bevel is not marked upon the brace, but the square is properly set for a pitch of 8 inches to the foot, or a one-third pitch. The square can now be placed upon the top of the brace, and the bevel marked. These examples are taken from "Bell's Carpentry," an excellent work that was very popular forty or fifty years ago because of its reliability and exhaustiveness. There have been many improvements in framing, however, since this book was made, still it contains some things that have never been improved on.

One style of mortise and tenon must not be overlooked, which is often employed in framing girts or girders, and that is the "bareface stub tenon," which I show at A in the illustration Fig. 244, Where it will be seen that at one side of the tenon there is a shoulder. The other side not having a shoulder is thus said to be barefaced. Since it does not pass right through the post, it is known as a stub tenon. This form of tenon is used where one surface of the girt is to be flush with that of a post, the other side of the girt being set back from that of the post (as shown).

In Figs. 245 and 246 I show a couple of examples of mixed, heavy and light framing. These will show how that style of work is done, and will, I am sure, prove of value to the learner.

It may not be out of place to say a few words on timbering floors, as the framer is often called upon to cut, frame and place all the necessary tim hers for the purpose, and to give him some idea of how the work should be done the following few illustrations and instructions are offered. In the first part of this work I gave a number of illus trations and methods of preparing timber for floors, so I will not now enter at much length into this subject, but briefly give a few examples of such work, as I know from experience will prove of the greatest value to the general workman:

Fig. 247.

A general system of floor framing in timber alone is shown in Fig. 247, the whole floor being of wood. Fig. 248 exhibits a timber floor intended for a double surface. The upper series carry the ceiling joists. At Fig. 249 I show how a framed floor, partly of wood and partly of iron, is usually put together in many localities. In Chicago and other places there is often a departure from this method, which is not always for the best. A double iron and timber floor is shown in Fig. 250, while a coal breeze or concrete floor with necessary steel girders is shown at Fig. 251. Fig. 252 shows a strongly reinforced concrete fireproof floor, capable of bearing great weights.

A few hints here regarding timbering floors, over and above what has been said, may not be out of place:

When ceilings are fixed direct to bridging joists that are thicker than 2% in., brandering fillets should be nailed on their bottom edges to fix the lathing to.

Ceiling joists in framed floors should be fixed to the binders. Notching or mortising the binder weakens it considerably.

Keep the ceiling joists % in. below the binder and counter lath the edge of the latter to afford key for plaster.

When the height is not sufficient to allow of the use of ceiling joists, notch the bridging joists 1 in. down on the binders, and lath and plaster direct. Also put in a row of plasterers' nails in the sides of the binder to form a key for the plaster, and plane and mould the visible portion of binder.

Every fourth or fifth bridge joist is well made 2 in. deeper than the rest, and the ceiling joists fixed thereto.

Pine is better than oak for ceiling joists.

To find the depth of ceiling joists, 2 in. thick, for any span, halve the bearing in feet; the result will be the depth in inches.

Ceiling joists should never exceed 24 in. in thickness, nor be less than 1% in. They should be spaced not more than 16 in. apart, center to center.

Ceiling joists should be thoroughly dry, or they will indicate their position first by dark and later by light stripes on the ceiling.

A flitched girder consists of a wrought iron plate placed between two timber flitches, and the three bolted together. The plate should be 14 in. within each edge of the wood, so that the weight shall not be all thrown on it when the wood has shrunk.

When pine or spruce plates are fixed to the sides of iron girders for the purpose of carrying the ends of joists, they may be secured with straps in place of bolts with advantage in points of strength and economy.

Scantlings for girders of Baltic fir; distance apart, 10 ft., center to center: and add an inch in each direction (breadth and depth) for every additional 2 ft. of span.

It is worse than useless to truss girders in their own depth.

Wood beams, when used as girders, should be cut down the middle, one of the flitches being reversed and the two then bolted together. This equalizes, if it does not increase, the strength, and at the same time affords an opportunity of seeing whether the heart is defective. The bolts should be placed mainly above the center line, and any placed below should be near the ends.

Wood girders for warehouses, factories, and similar buildings, are better unwrought. If it is desired to paint them, they should be cased with worked pine linings, fixed to V2 m-firring pieces.

The formula for the strength of timber girders

'. w n b d2

is $W = C\,T$

Where W = breaking weight in cwts. L = span in feet b = breadth in inches d = depth of girder in inches C = constant = 5 for oak, pitch pine, and birch = 4 for southern pine.

Load at center and beam supported only.

The maximum strength of a timber beam is obtained when the breadth is to the depth as 5 is to 7.

The illustration shown at Fig. 253 makes plain the method of constructing a double floor. The binder rests on a wall or posts. This makes a fine floor, and is in a measure sound proof.

Figs. 254, 255, 256 and 257, which are borrowed from *Architecture and Building*—old series—will convey to the reader a number of excellent ideas as to the combination of iron and wood in floor framing.

Fig. 258 shows the manner usually adopted in preparing the floor timbers around a hearth, chimney breast, stair well hole, or openings for trap doors or similar work. The trimmers and headers are made with heavier timbers than the joists, and the tail beams are let into the headers with either plain or tusk-tenons. Tusk-tenons, of course, are the best, but entail much labor and care. A tusktenon with a run-over top, is shown in Fig. 259.

This makes a good clean joint for running over a girt or bearing timber, and can be nailed together over the joint as shown, thus holding the work so that it cannot spread. The tenon is shown at A.

There are various shapes of tusk-tenons, some of which are shown in the foregoing examples. I give below herewith a brief description of what I think makes the best kind of a tenon:

The usual rule for cutting a common tenon is to make it one-third the width of the timber and this rule should be followed as far as possible in designing a tusk-tenon. The projection of the tenon from the beam out of which it is cut is called its root, and the surfaces immediately adjacent to its root on the sides are called the shoulders.

The tusk-tenon was devised in order to give the tenon a deep bearing at the root, without greatly increasing the size of the mortise. Making the
Fig. 258.
mortise unduly large would, of course, weaken the girder. The desired deep bearing is secured by adding below the tenon a tusk having a shoulder which in trimmer work penetrates to a depth about one-sixth the thickness of the joist. Above the tenon is formed what is called a "horn," the lower end of which penetrates to the same extent as the tusk. By this arrangement the strength of the tenon is greatly increased as compared with the common form, while the mortise is not made very much larger. In order to hold the narts together the tenon is projected through the girder and pinned on the outside as shown in the sketches.

So much for a description of the tusk-tenon, as it is theoretically, and as illustrated in Fig. 261. Many times, however, the tusk-tenon is attempted upon the lines shown in Fig. 260. For example, if the beams are 10 inches deep, it is placed so as to leave 6 in. beneath. This does not secure the maximum of strength. The tenon is made square on the shoulder, which is not the best that might be done and has below the root the bearing indicated by A in the sketch.

The object in view with this joint, where applied to small timbers, as, for example, headers in floor beams, as well as in heavy framing, is to secure a perfect bearing at all points. In the application of it to floor beams the special object is to weaken the trimmer as little

as possible.

It is scarcely necessary to remind the readers that a beam weighed and supported like a trimmer has the fibers on the bottom in tension, while those at the top are in compression. If this is conceded, then it becomes evident that whatever is to be cut out of the beam ought to be cut out as near the center as possible. The root of the tenon should pierce the beam at a point as nearly on the neutral axis as may be. The nearer it is placed to the bottom of the beam, that is to be connected with the trimmer, the less likely the tenon is to split off, and as near the middle of the beam from top to bottom as possible, is the proper point for the tenon. There is some liability of the tenon splitting off, however, wherever it is placed, and it is for this reason that the shoulder D, as shown in Fig. 261, is introduced. The bearing E also helps to strengthen the construction.

Fig. 260 is not an ideal tenon, so in practice it is always better to employ tenon shown at 261.

One very important feature in heavy framing is the construction of wood centers for turning over brick or stone arches, and I purpose giving at this point some examples of centers most in common use, and a few suitable for bridge and other large works.

Before describing the types of center in common use it will be well to consider the points that must be observed in their construction. The principles that are enunciated below apply to most temporary structures, but are here intended to apply chiefly to centering. (1) Absolute rigidity of the struc ture is required. (2) A wide margin of safety in the resistance of the material and fastenings of joints. (3) Fastenings should be easy of application and removal, and yet perfectly reliable. (4) The structure must be economically designed, which does not mean always to use as little material as possible, but rather that it shall sustain the minimum amount of damage in jointing and framing, so as to allow of re-use for similar purposes when the sizes are suitable, or conversion into timber for other purposes. (5) Joints must be so arranged as to transmit

stresses directly with the least possible tendency to slide when under compression, and where necessary the fastenings of the joints must be such as to allow of the stresses being severed without movement of such joints during the loading of the center. Thus, when an arch is being erected, if of a semi-circular or semielliptical outline, the first few stones or bricbs will produce no stress in the center, for the tendency of the blocks to slide is resisted by the friction between the surfaces until the angle of repose of the material is reached. After passing this point, the center becomes quickly loaded and the compression at the haunches is severe, and being loaded symmetrically from the two sides, produces a strong tendency to lift at the crown, which the center has to resist. What is required is an arrangement of trussing the ribs, or separate vertical frames supporting the lagging, that will resist this deformation, and further, that of the continued loading up to the insertion of the key clock. To attain resistance and rigidity so as to overcome these difficulties requires careful consideration in large centers. The center as a whole consists of the supports, the curved trussed ribs, and the cover or lagging which the ribs support.

First, as regards the ribs, these should be trussed frames of the required outline placed at 3, 4 or 5 feet centers, according to the weight of the arch, strength of lagging and timbers; each rib 01 bent receiving direct support. The construction of the rib may be accomplished in one of three ways: (a) It may have the curve built up in two or more thicknesses; (b) it may be of solid material, connecting the struts, its outer surface cut to the curve; or (c) the frame may be trussed to the outline very approximately, and the curve formed by shaped packings nailed to the other members. The general practice appears to be to use (a) in two thicknesses, for small centers, simply nailing or screwing the sections together; (b) for large civil engineering structures; and (c) also for the latter work and for arches of moderate span that are near the semicircular outline. We may consider (c) as a modification of (b). But there is a great advantage in using the built-up eurve for centers of comparatively large size, especially where the whole rib can be built up and then raised into position, because of the fact that if the joints between the lengths of material are radial (normal) to the curve, the rib, apart from trussing, is in a great measure self-sustaining, its form being that of an arch, and, therefore, capable of sustaining a load. The writer knows of some cases where built-up curved ribs (without trussing), merely lagged and braced, have been successfully used to build segmental arches of small rise over moderate spans. This advantage of the built-up rib is increased if three thicknesses of material are used, and $y2$ in. bolts instead of spikes employed at the joints. Moreover, the ribs are then very easily taken to pieces, the bolts used again for any suitable purpose, and the lengths of curve either re-cut for similar purposes or converted to other uses.

The following rules and definitions regarding centers and centering will be found quite useful to the workman and are inserted here for his guidance and consideration:

'' Centers are temporary wooden structures upon which arches are built.

For convenience of reference they may be classified according to construction, as turning pieces, rib centers, laminated, or "built up," framed and trussed, close-lagged, and sundry special varieties designated in connection with the purpose for which they are used, such as dome, circle on circle, groin, and sheeting centers.

Centers being required purely for temporary purposes should be designed so as to injure the material as little as possible, with a view to its subsequent use for other purposes.

This condition often necessitates the employment of larger timbers than are actually required to meet the stresses occasioned by the load.

But it is a good fault in centering to have the timber "too heavy," as in extensive works such as railway arches or large vaults, stresses sometimes develop in unexpected directions.

Every effort should be made to transmit the load to the ground, directly, by vertical supports; and if the distance is great these should be braced.

Inclined supports, as sometimes used, to give clear way for traffic, are apt to shrink and become loose, riding on the dogs, and so throw themselves out of bearing if not watched.

The above does not apply to arches whose abutments are piers. In this case it is better to throw the weight of the centering upon the footings, or some part of the pier, otherwise when the center is struck, and the extra weight of the arches thrown on them, they may settle unequally.

They must be constructed in such manner that their shape will not be altered by the stresses induced by the load, which, of course, are continually altering in amount and direction as the work proceeds. This requirement is best met by bracing and counter-bracing.

It is inadvisable, except in the case of very heavy centers, to employ mortise and tenon joints in the construction, as, apart from the expense of these, it is requisite, in order to obtain good results, that the timbers should be "true," and as this condition is not essential for any other purpose in the construction, it is unwise to so design it when other and simpler joints will answer the purpose equally well.

Large centers should be *so* constructed that they may be readily set up, and it is better to build them on the site, piece by piece, having previously fitted and marked them, than to build them complete on the ground, and sling them into position with a crane. This slinging will often disarrange the braces and distort the ribs. This refers to "Builders' Centers" only. Engineers centers, usually more elaborately braced and tied with iron rods, being not affected thereby.

Centers should also be capable of easy striking and ready readjustment. These requirements are usually met by introducing pairs of folding wedges between the supports and the lower bearings of the center. There is always a danger of these wedges, whilst being driven back, suddenly shooting away

and leaving the center unsupported. This may be avoided by using three wedges, as shown at Fig. 286. Then if either the top or bottom one is driven out, a pair still remain to take the bearing, and "set up" again if required. An elaboration of this method is shown in Fig. 287, a continuous wedge, used sometimes for heavy centers. It is impossible for this form to slip, and it can be locked in position when set up by a key driven in one of the slots.

Screw jacks may also be employed to obtain regular easing in doubtful cases of vaulting or restorative work.

Another point to remember in designing centers, is that there may be projections below the springing, such as cap or neck moldings, that will prevent the lowering of the center if due allow ance is-not made for them; an example of this is given in Figs. 268 and 277. The tie-piece should be made a little shorter than the clear distance between the projections, and raised above the springing to a point where it will cut the ihtrados of the arch.

The tail-pieces, completing the center down to the springing, are made up separately and inserted after the body is set up. These tail-pieces would not be required for a masonry arch, as the haunch voussoirs do not take a bearing on the center until their bed joints exceed an angle of 32 degrees with the horizontal. This is due to the friction of the stone on its bed preventing its sliding, unless the angle of the bed is in excess of that mentioned.

it may also be noted that the whole weight of any arch stone is not taken by the centering until the stone is in such a position on it that a vertical line drawn through its center of gravity would pass on the outside of its bed.

It follows that during the construction of the arch, the load gradually increases from the springing to the crown; and that in a semi-circular arch, when about half way up between springing and crown, the load will have a tendency to force the haunches in and spring the crown up. This demonstrates the necessity (a) of making the center stronger in the middle than at the haunches, as a greater weight will have to be carried by that part; and (b) either that the stress from the haunches be taken direct to the ground by supports at the feet of the braces, as in Figs. 271 and 277, or where no support is available from below, at the middle of the span by framing the feet of the haunchbraces into the foot of a king post, which will counteract the tendency of the latter to rise, and then to meet the stress at the crown that will come later by taking braces from the head of the king post to the end of the tie-piece, directing the stress to the supports at the springing as shown in Fig. 272.

It is safer to increase the number of ribs than the thickness of the lagging. It is difficult to lay down any rule for the spacing of the ribs, as the conditions vary in almost every case, but they must be close enough to prevent any individual lag yielding under the load, and so crippling the surface of the arch.

It must be remembered that the bricklayer requires to pass his plumb rule and lines across the face of the work, and over the openings, so that the ends of the lagging should be kept within the line of the finished work.

Fig. 263.

It is a convenience to let the lags run over the ribs about 1% in., so that they can be trimmed as required.

Laggings for brickwork should be spaced not more than 1% in. apart. For masonry they can be spaced according to the length of the voussoirs used. A bearing at each edge is sufficient. Frequently where the voussoirs exceed two feet in length, lagging is dispensed with altogether, the stones being supported by blocks or wedges arranged as the work proceeds. This method is shown in Fig. 277.

Oak is often used for wedges, but maple is a better wood, being much less likely to split; it is also naturally smooth and slips well. If oak is used, its surface should be soaped or black-leaded. The wood should be dry, and if machine cut, a fine tooth saw should be used, or if cut with a coarse saw, the faces should be planed. The thin end should not be less than % in. thick, and the corners

of both ends "dubbed" off, as shown in Fig. 286, to prevent splitting.

"Wedges should be driven parallel to the abutments, i. e., across the ribs and have a block nailed behind them to prevent running back.

The turning piece, Fig. 262, is cut out of a piece 2 in. by 4 in.; it is used for the outside arches of door and window openings, of slight rise, and half a brick thick. For thicker walls the rib center, Fig. 263, is used. This is formed by shaping two boards, about 1 in. thick, to the curve, keeping them at a proper distance apart by stretchers, S, nailed on their lower edges, and covering the curved edges with lagging pieces, L, about $iy2$ in. by % in- at intervals of % in. for ordinary work.

When the rise of a center is small in comparison to its span, it is inconvenient to describe its curve with a radius rod, and the method shown in Fig. 264 may be adopted. Take a piece of board of convenient size and draw a line across it from edge to edge, equal in length to the span of the arch required; at the center of this line draw a perpendicular equal in length to the rise, draw a line from this point, b, to the springing point, a, and cut the ends off beyond the line; the portion cut off is shown by dotted lines in the sketch. Two nails are driven into the piece from which the segment is to be cut, at a distance apart equal to the span, as at a-c, and the templet placed in the position shown in Fig. 264, with a pencil held at point b; if the board is now moved around towards a, keeping it pressed against the nails, one-half the curve will be described, and on turning over and repeating the process the other half may be completed.

An alternative method is shown in Fig. 264, suitable for very flat arches. Lay off the rise, and span, perpendicular to each other, as a, b and c, upon any convenient surface; draw the cord line a c, lay the board from which the templet is to be cut in a suitable position over these lines, and reproduce the line a c upon it; also draw the line e d parallel to a b; next cut the board to this triangular shape, as shown by the shaded portion; then if nails are driven in the

board to be cut at points a and c, and the templet moved around against them, the curve will be described by a pencil held at point e, as shown by the dotted line.

When the rise is more than the width of a board will accommodate, a variation of this method may be used. Into the board or boards from which the rib is to be cut three nails are driven, as at a, b, c, Fig. 265, arranged so that a-c shall equal the span and b the rise, then place two strips of wood against the nails as shown, crossing at the crown, and fix them together; a third piece nailed across to form a triangle will keep them in position, if the nail at the apex is withdrawn and a pencil substituted; when the triangle is moved around as before described, the curve will be produced. One of the legs of the triangle should be twice the length from a to b.

A built-up center is shown in Figs. 266 and 267; the ribs in this variety are formed in two thicknesses, the laminae being nailed together in short lengths, the abutting joints of each layer meeting in the center of the other. These abutment joints should not be less than 4 in. long, and should radiate from the center of the curve. The length of the segments is determined by the amount of the curve that can be cut out of a 9 in. board. The two longer layers of the rib at the springing are cut off at the top edge of the tie-pieces, and form with the upper layer, which runs down to its bottom edge, a rebate, in which the tie rests. The layer running down is nailed to the tie. The tie-piece may be from 1 in. by 7 in. to 1% in. by 9 in., according to the span. The braces, of similar scantling, should radiate from the center, and be shouldered slightly upon the same side of the tie-piece that the ribs run over; their upper ends are nailed on the side of the layer of the rib, and take a bearing under the edges of the other. This form of center may be safely used for spans up to 12 ft., but although sometimes used for greater, they are not to be recommended owing to the numerous joints, and the possibility of splitting the segments in nailing.

The framed center, Fig. 268, is better adapted for spans between 12 ft. and 20 ft. The ribs are solid, out of 2 in. or 3 in. by 9 in., as the span is less or more, and if this is not wide enough to get the curve out, in four or five lengths, must be made up to the required width, with similar pieces spiked on the back. The ends near the springing are shouldered out m-on each side to sit on the tie-pieces, which are in pairs; the upper ends have slot mortises cut in them to receive the tenons on the braces (see Figs. 269 and 270). The lower ends of the braces are shouldered in a manner similar to the ribs. The ends in the ties are fixed with coach screws, the upper ends by dogs.

A trussed center of economical construction is shown in Fig. 271, consisting of a triangulated frame of quartering, used as a support to the ribs. The foundation frame may take the form of either a king or queen post truss, as the span and number of braces required may indicate; but whatever the form, as previously mentioned, the stresses should be directed to the points of support, in this case three.

The joints are formed by notching the ends of the braces into the ties, and keeping them in position by means of dogs. No tenons are used, as from the construction all the members will be in compression; short puncheons should be used under the joints of the ribs, as shown at PP. This form may be used safely for brick arches up to 25 ft. span, but must be supported in the middle. When this course is not possible a trussed and framed center, similar to Fig. 272, may be employed. This is a very strong construction, espe cially suitable for masonry arches in which considerable cross strains, due to the slower manipulation of the load, have to be met. Here it will be seen that the haunch loads are directed to the foot of the king post, and not to the tie; from that point it is directed by way of the struts D to the supports at the end of the tie. These same struts, D, also take the crown load. The king post, tie piece and struts D are all made solid, the latter passing between the struts E, into which they are notched slightly, to stiffen them (see detail, Fig. 275). Packing pieces are used at the upper ends of the struts E, to bring the ribs up to the bearing (see Fig. 276), the whole fastened together with spikes or coach screws. The ends of the ribs at crown and springing are sunk in about % in. (see Fig. 274), the lower ends being spiked through the back. The lags are 2 in. by 3 in., spaced ac cording to requirements, about two-thirds of the length of the stone from the bed joint of each voussoir will be found the best position. The ribs are spaced at 3 ft. 6 in. apart. The lags in the example are shown notched into the backs of the ribs $y2$ in.; this method is often adopted when the center is built in situ, and the length of the arch is such as to require several ribs. The two end ribs should have a radius rod fixed on the tiepiece, to be swept round the circumference, and the lags can be brought into the line of curve by adjusting the depth of notch. When the end pair are correct, a line sprung through, or a straight edge applied, will give the depth of the intermediate notching.

A trussed center for a large span is illustrated by Figs. 277 and 283. Figs. 283 and 284 are details of the construction..

Centers of the above description are generally constructed as follows: a chalk line diagram, complete, and full size, is laid down on a suitable platform or floor, the timber from which the segments of the ribs are to be cut are laid in position over the curve alternately, and the joints marked with a straight edge, radiating from the center; or, in the case of elliptic or parabolic arches, drawn normal to the curve at the points where the joints occur (see n, Fig. 282). When the joints are cut the segments are laid down and nailed together, a radius rod is then swept round to mark the curve, or in segmental arches the triangle, Fig. 282, may he used; the pieces are then separated and cut, again laid down with spikes driven temporarily around their periphery to keep them in place; the struts and ties are then laid over them in position, and the lines for the shouldering and notching drawn on; each joint should have a chisel mark made on the pieces to identify them, and the joints being made, the whole can be fitted together, nailed up and bolted, then taken to pieces ready for re-erection in situ.

Close lagged centers for various purposes are shown in Figs. 278 and 280 and 284. The surface of these is required to be finished more accurately than in the ordinary center, because the bricklayer sets out the plans Of his courses thereon, and thus obtains the shape of the voussoirs. The lagging is nailed closely round the ribs, and brought into the curve afterwards, with the plane.

The profile line being obtained either by radius rod or templet. In the case of Dome or Niche centers, a reverse templet affords the readiest guide for shaping the surface.

A circle on circle center, when semicircular in elevation, may be constructed as shown in Figs. 274 to 278. Two ribs are cut to the plan curve, and upon each edge of these narrow vertical laggings, rather closely spaced, and thin enough to bend easily to the curve, are nailed. The bottom rib is placed at the springing, the other about half way between it and the crown, when

Fig. 280.

this side lagging is fixed, a radius rod shaped as in Fig. 277, and set out so that the distance between the pivot A and the middle of the V notch is equal to the radius of the required arch, less the thickness of the soffit lagging; is mounted on a temporary stretcher, C, at the middle of the springing; this is swept round the lagging on each side, a pencil being held loosely in the V notch, thus obtaining the outline of the elevation curve. (Of course if the soffit were splayed the inner radius would be shorter, but struck from the same level as the outer.) The boards are cut square through to the lines and the cross lagging nailed to their ends, as shown in the section.

When the plan curve is flat, such as would occur in a narrow opening in a large circular wall, the vertical lagging may be omitted and the center built as shown in Figs. 278 and 282, plain vertical ribs being employed, and the lags allowed to overhang sufficiently to form, the plan curves. They require to be rather stouter than usual to ensure stiffness.

There are two ways in which centering for intersecting vaults may be constructed: first, when the vault is not of great span, a "barrel" or continuous center is made for the main vault, long enough to run about two feet beyond each side of the intersecting vault. The centers of the smaller vaults are then made with the lagging overhanging the rib at one end, the two centers are then placed on a level surface and brought together in their correct relative positions, and the loose ends of lagging scribed to fit the contour of the main center, and then nailed thereto.

This method, however, is unsuitable for vaults of large span, as the lagging would be liable to sink at the intersection through the absence of support. The second method, shown in Figs. 281 and 283, is then adopted; a rectangular frame is first constructed equal in length to the proposed center, and in width to the clear span between the walls; this frame is halved together at the angles, as shown at E, Fig. 283, and forms a firm base for fixing the ribs to; a similar frame is made and fixed underneath for the cross vault, and ribs of the requisite curvature are set up at the four ends, also at the intersecting line or groin, being secured firmly at the base.

The groin ribs are made in two thicknesses for convenience of beveling, the angle of the seating being a re-entrant one.

The method of producing the bevel is explained elsewhere. The lagging of the cylindric center should be fixed first and worked off true with the aid of a plane and straight-edge; a thin straight lath should then be bent round over the center of the groin rib, and a pencil line drawn down its edge;-the ends of the lagging being trimmed off to it with a chisel held plumb; this will give the proper intersection for the main lags, and when jthese latter are cut to fit their true outline at the intersection may be obtained by marking on their ends with a pencil drawn down the surface of the

cylinder. A templet, obtained as described below, applied at the ends will give the profile at the extremities, and each lag can be placed to fit before nailing on.

To find the space of a groin rib when the shape of penetrating vault is given: First, by means of ordinates; divide the semi-circular rib, A, Fig. 283, into a number of parts, as at 1, 2, 3, 4, 5; draw perpendiculars from these to the springing line x, and produce the lines to cut the plan of the center of groin rib, in a, b, c, d, x; erect perpendiculars at these points to the plan line, d-f, and mark off on them heights to correspond with the similarly marked heights in the section, Fig. 283; these will give points in the curve, which may be drawn by driving in nails at the points and bending a thin lath round them. The curve may, however, be drawn quicker by a trammel, taking the height, x-, for the minor axis, and the length, d-x, for the major axis. When a properly constructed trammel is not at hand, its principle may be utilized in the following manner: To draw an ellipse without a trammel—Let A, C, B, Fig. 284, represent a board upon which it is desired to draw a semi-ellipse, joint the edge, A, B, straight, draw a line in the center, square with the edge, as C, produce it across another piece of board resting against the first, to D; then mark 'off, on a straight lath from one end, the semi-major and semi-minor axes; in other words, the rise and half-span of the arch. Keeping these two points upon the lines, A, B, and C, D, arrange the lath in Various positions, as shown by dotted lines in Fig. 284, and pencil lines made at its end will give points on the curve.

To find the shape of the ribs for the main center, Fig. 283, ftom the points a', b', c', d', x', in plan, draw lines parallel to the edge of the center, intersecting the seat of the end rib in points a", b", c", d", x"; along these lines set off heights equal to the corresponding ordinates in Fig. 281, and draw the outline of the rib through them, as at C, Fig. 284.

To find joint line and direction for braces in elliptic centers, see Fig. 284.

First find the focal points, with radius equal to half the span a b. Describe an arc from center c, cutting the major axis a b in f f; these are the foci. To find the joint line or normal from any point in the curve as n (fixed conveniently for length of stuff), draw straight lines to the foci; bisect the contained angle, as shown by a line drawn through the point n and the center of the constructive arc. This line is a normal or perpendicular to the curve at the point in question, and indicates the direction of joint and braces.

The method of bevelling a groin rib for the purpose of obtaining a level seating for the lagging is shown in Fig. 283. Let c, d, b represent the plan of one-half of a groin rib similar to H, x, Fig. 281, and C, d', the elevation, which may also represent the mould or templet; a, e, f, g is the piece of board from which the rib is to be cut, on the face side of the board draw the full line, C, d', by aid of the mould, cut the ends square with each other, as a, e, and d, g, then apply the bevel as found at d in plan from point d' across the bottom edge, square a line across the top end at C, and apply the mould on the other side of the board, as shown by the dotted line with its lower end at the bevel line and its upper end to the level line from point C. If the rib is cut to these two lines, and a similar one made the reverse hand and nailed together, as shown in Fig. 281, its edge will lie in the planes of the directions of the intersecting vaults.

The methods shown in the following descriptions and illustrations further affords very convenient means of jointing, for the struts can always be made to meet at points such as A or B in Fig. 289, making possible either a mortise-andtenon or a bridle joint, without cutting into the rib; for taking either of the two positions given, the crossing of the sections of the curve provided the necessary entering or receiving portion of the joint, leaving only one-half of the joint to be worked on the strut. In the solid-rib type, the curve is made up of lengths of solid material, with the joints between each part of the strut connections, thereby becoming separate members to the frame. The curve itself has no resistance apart from its connection with the struts. The jointing in this case is more of a permanent na-i ture.

The arrangement of the members of the rib, so as to give internal support to the curve, depends on conditions that will be readily noted as the diagrams are perused. If the span and outline be such that the rise is not great, the struts may all be brought directly on to the tie, and concentrated on the intermediate supports, as shown in Fig. 290. This type should have solid ribs jointed at the points A, B, C, etc., as shown (for details of which see Figs. 290 and 291). If, however, the rise be great, either a flat member must be bolted across the face of the rib so as to shorten the struts effectively, or, better, the type shown in Fig. 293 can be adopted, which shows the method of arranging the members more suitably. The struts are much shorter, and can therefore be lighter. A great resistance to lifting at the crown is obtained, and if necessary the intermediate supports can be dispensed with. Further, the direct supports to the curve may be all normals, or their equivalent, for this latter condition is satisfied if a pair of struts meet at an equal incli nation (Fig. 292). Fig. 293 gives the elevation in line diagram, and Fig. 294 gives the full details of the construction, span 30 ft. The rib is here built up in three one and a half inches stuff. In both Figs. 289 and 293 the tie is double, of 2x9 in. material. Fig. 293 fulfills the requirement of a good center, and therefore this form may with advantage be generally adopted and modified in the internal trussing as the span increases.

Elliptical arches of long spans are somewhat more difficult to deal with, and I present the following merely to enable workmen to deal with centers of this kind, having a span from 30 to 100 feet.

Large centers for civil engineering structures, such as bridges crossing rivers in several spans, are scarcely within our scope, these requiring special treatment according to circumstances. But we may with advantage just note

on the general forms of centers that are adopted for comparatively flat elliptical arches, together with a modification for a greater rise. Fig. 295 is the general form. It has many points of support, therefore little tendency to give at the crown. The whole of the material is of large size, 6 in. by 6 in. being the minimum, and for the platform whole

Fig. 297.

timbers 12 in. by 12 in. receive the vertical posts. For heavier work and wider spans, the construction given in Fig. 298 is well adapted. Details in

Figs. 296 to 300 show the construction of joints which applies throughout. This is built in two tiers, keeping the struts comparatively short, and effectively distributes pressure to the points of support. The secondary horizontal member is large enough to clasp the curved rib at the ends (see Fig. 301), and the whole of the joints are housed or tenoned and strapped where necessary, and as shown in details. Transverse and longitudinal bracing is freely used in the manner pre viously described, and by careful arrangement and sufficient bracing in vertical planes the necessity for strap connections can be reduced to a minimum. For heavy arches such as these the centers are struck by the introduction of lifting jacks or sand boxes, the latter being especially suited to the purpose. They are arranged to contain fine dry sand, with means of escape for the sand as needed, so that the center may be lowered easily and gradually, and to any required amount within the provided limits.

I show at Figs. 302, 303, 304 and 305 four examples of centers in situ, carrying the brick or stone work, as the case may be; Fig. 302 shows a center for a small span. It consists of a trussed frame, of which A is the tie, B the principal, or, and F a strut. The center is carried by the piles D, on the top of which is a capping piece E, extending across the opening; and the wedge blocks are interposed betwixt it and the tie-beam.

Fig. 302.

as its outer edge is curved to the contour of the arch, it is called the felloe, C the post or puncheon,

Fig. 303 shows center for a small span for an elliptical arch.

Fig. 304 shows a center with intermediate supports and simple framing, consisting of two trusses formed on the puncheons over the intermediate supports as king-posts, and subsidiary trusses for the haunches, with struts from their center parallel to the main struts. This is an excellent design for a center carrying a segmental flat arch having a large span.

Fig. 305 shows a system of supporting a large semi-elliptical center arch rib from the intermediate supports by radiating struts, which, with modifications to suit the circumstances of the case, have been very extensively adopted in many large works connected with railroads in this country and Europe. The struts abut at their upper end on straining pieces, or apron pieces, as they are sometimes called, which are bolted to the rib, and serve to strengthen it. The ends of the transverse braces are seen at a a.

The examples and details of centers given in the foregoing are quite sufficient to enable the foreman to lay-out, and execute any job of building a center that may confront him; and at this point we leave the subject of centers, and take up another important one, namely, that of timber roof framing. While I propose discussing timber roofs and trusses in general in this department, it is not intended to deal with roof coverings further than may be necessary to make the instructions and suggestions given herewith intelligible and so that they may be understood by every workman who can read.

There are a few general rules governing timber roof framing the workman should always have in mind when building or designing a roof of any kind, a few of which I submit; and which I hope will prove of sufficient importance to be remembered: 1. Every construction should be a little stronger than "strong enough." 2. Roofs should neither be too heavy nor too slight; both extremes should be rigorously avoided.

3. Flat-pitched roofs are not so strong as higher pitched ones. 4. Suitable pitches

of roofs for various coverings are: Copper, lead, or zinc, 6 degrees; corrugated iron, 8 degrees; tiles and slates, 33 degrees to 45 degrees. 5. Approximate weight of roofs per square: The timber framing, 5% cwt.; Countess slates, 6% cwt.; add for 1 in. pine or hemlock boarding, *2y2* cwt.; plain tiles, 14 cwt. ; 7 lb. lead, 6 cwt.; 1-32 in. zinc, *iy2* cwt. 6. The construction should be able to withstand an additional weight of 30 cwt. per square for wind pressure. 7. When the carpentry forming the roof of a building is of great extent, instead of being injurious to the stability of the walls or points of support, it should be so designed that it will strengthen and keep them together. 8. Forms of roofs for various spans should couple, up to 11 ft.; couple close, to 14 ft.; collar, to 17 ft.; king post, to 30 ft.; queen post, to 46 ft.; queen and princess, to 75 ft. 9. Roof trusses should be prepared from sound, dry timber, white or red pine, free from large knots, sap, and shakes, all parts to hold sizes shown in figured dimensions, and all joints to be stub-tenoned and to fit square to shoulders. Tiebeam should be cambered % in. in 10 ft., and straps and bolts be of best wrought-iron. No spikes should be used in the construction except for fixing cleats. 10. Tie beams should be supported every 15 ft. 11. Struts should be taken as nearly as possible under bearing of purlin. 12. The straining beams in spans of 50 ft. and upwards require support, and a king bolt or post should be introduced. 13. To find the thickness of king post trusses, divide the span by five and call the quotient inches. Assume 9 in. and 5 in. as the standard depth of tie beams and principal rafter respectively for 20 ft. span; add 1 in. to each for every additional 5 ft. of span. King posts' and struts to be square. 14. To find the thickness of queen post trusses, divide the span by eight and call the quotient inches; if odd parts result, add 1 in. for tiles, and for slates take off the fraction. Taking the standard depth of tie beam and principal for 32 ft. span to be 11 in. and 6 in. respectively, add 1 in. to each for every 5 ft. of additional span. The struts and body of the queens to be

made square. 15. Wall plates are used to distribute the weight of roof timbers, and also to act as ties to the walls. For this reason tie-beams should be cogged to the plates, the latter dove-tail-halved at the angle, and dove-tail-scarfed in longitudinal joints. Wall plates in roofs should be creosoted or otherwise protected against rot, and bedded in cement knocked up stiff. 16. Purlins should be cogged or notched on to principal rafters and not framed between them. When cogged or notched they will carry nearly twice as much as when framed. 17. The available strength of tie beams is that of the uncut fibres, and, therefore, mortises should be shallow, and all notching be avoided. 18. Scarfs in tie beams should be made between the points of support, and not directly under them, as any mortises or bolt-holes at these points reduce the strength of the beam. 19. Dragon ties should be provided at the angles of hipped roofs to take. the thrust of the hips and to tie in the ends of wall plates. It is best that the hip should be deep enough to birdsmouth over the angle brace. 20. Wind braces, which are diagonal ties in roofs open at the ends, as in railway stations, to withstand the overturning or racking pressure of the wind, may be of timber framed between the purlins, or iron rods running from the head of one truss to the foot of the next. 21. Hip rafters, being deeper than the common rafters, are visible inside when the roof is ceiled, and should be covered with a casing. 22. Hips should stand perfectly at an angle of 45 degrees with the plates on plan, as by this arrangement the rafters on either side are equal in length, inclination, and bevel at the ends, making the construction both symmetrical and economical. 23. When the span is of such extent that the end purlin is longer than those of the side bays, a half truss should be introduced at the center of the end, with its tie-beam trimmed into the end transverse truss. 24. All the abutment joints in a framed truss should be at right angles with the direction of thrust, and when this is parallel with the edges of the member, the shoulders may be cut square with the back of such member.

25. To resist the racking movement in roofs, an effectual plan consists in the employment of wind ties of iron. These extend usually from the head of one principal to the foot of the next principal, but one on the same side of the roof, and again from the head of this latter principal to the foot of the first one, so that the tie rods cross one another in the form of an X. It is difficult to estimate the stress which will come upon these ties; but very small sections, say from % in. to % in., will generally suffice for the purpose. 26. The amount of horizontal thrust at the foot of a principal rafter depends partly upon the weight of the truss and the loads or stresses which it has to sustain, and partly upon the inclination of the rafter. The lower the pitch of the roof, the greater is the proportion of thrust to weight, so that for roofs natter than quarter pitch stronger tie beams will be necessary. 27. In queen post trusses the position of the queen posts may vary. Generally, however, when there are no rooms in the roof, they are placed at one-third of the span from the wall. 28. When rooms are formed in queen post roofs, the distance between the queens may conveniently be half the span or more, but in such instances the depth of tie-beam should be increased. 29. The best form of roof truss to be used in any situation may be determined by the following considerations: (1) The parts of the truss between the points of support should not be so long as to haVe any tendency to bend under the thrust —therefore, the lengths of the parts under compression should not exceed twenty times their smallest dimensions; (2) The distance apart of the purlins should not be so great as to necessitate the use of either purlins or rafters too large for convenience or economy; (3) The tie-beam should be supported at such small intervals that it need not be too large for economy. 30. It has been found by experience that these objects can be attained by limiting the distance between the points of support on the principal rafter to 8 ft., and upon the tie-beam to 15 ft. 31. To determine the form of roof truss for any given span, it is, therefore necessary first to decide

the pitch, then roughly to draw the principal rafters in position, ascertain their length, divide them into portions 8 ft. long, and place a strut under each point of division. By this it will be seen that a king post truss is adapted for a roof, with principal rafters 16 ft. long—i. e. , those having a span of 30 ft. 32. A queen post truss would be adapted to a roof with principals 24 ft. long—i. e. , about 45 ft. span. For greater spans, with longer principals, compound roofs are required. 33. In the case of a roof with three spans, subject to the effects of lateral wind pressure, when supported on side walls with intermediate columns, where the situation does not permit either the addition of buttresses or of anchorage in these side walls, the horizontal reaction of the wind pressure may be taken by bracing the intermediate columns to a concrete foundation. 34. The shoulders at the foot of king and queen post trusses should be cut short when framed, to prevent the tie-beam sagging when the truss has settled, the usual allowance being $y2$ in. for each 10 ft. of span. 35. Scarfing requires great accuracy in execution, because if the indents do not bear equally, the greater part of the strength will be lost; hence it is improper to use very complicated forms. 36. The simplest form of joint is, as a rule, the strongest; complicated joints are to be admired more for the ingenuity and skill of the carpenter in contriving and fitting than for their strength of construction. 37. In scarfing, when bolts are used, about four times the depth of the timber is the usual length for a scarf. 38. Scarfed tension joints should be fitted with folding wedges, so as to admit of their being tightened up. The wedges should be of oak or other suitable hard wood. 39. Galvanized iron bolts do not act upon oak, either in sea or in fresh water, when care has been taken not to remove the zinc in driving them. 40. In calculating the weight of roof coverings, about 10 per cent should be added to weight of tiles for moisture. 41. Valley boards are used sometimes on small roofs in place of valley rafters. The main roof is continued through in the usual way, and a 1 in. by 9 in. board

is nailed up the rafters on each side at the intersection of the two roofs to receive the feet of the jack rafters. 42. To carry ridge boards, the purlins, ridge, and wall-plates should oversail gable ends 12 in. or 18 in., and short purlin pieces should be cogged on the principals every 3 ft. for additional fixings when the barges are very wide and heavy. 43. Finals are fixed on the end of the ridge board with stub tenons, drawbore pinned, paint being applied to the tenon. 44. All openings in a roof should be trimmed; that is, cross-pieces should be framed between the two rafters bounding the opening to carry the ends of the intermediate ones cut away. 45. The trimmer, as the cross bearer is called, is fixed square with the pitch of the roof, tusktenoned and wedged at the ends, and the stopped rafters are stubtenoned into it. 46. When the opening is for a chimney, provision must be made for a gutter at the top. Bearers, 3 in. by 2 in., are nailed to the sides of the rafters, level, with their ends abutting against the chimney stack; a 1 in. gutter board is nailed on these, and a 9 in. lear board at the side on the rafters. About 3 in. up the slope a % in. tilting fillet is fixed, and over this the lead is dressed, the other side being taken up the back of the chimney for 6 in., and covered with an apron flashing. 47. Other openings, such as those for skylights and trapdoors, are trimmed in the same way, and covered with wrought linings or stout frames, dove-tailed at the angles, called curbs. 48. Sizes of wall plates for 20 ft. span, $4/2$ in. by 3 in.; for 30 ft., 6 in. by 4 in.; for 40 ft., $7y2$ in. by 5 in. 49. Ground floor wall plates are best of oak, and a damp course should be put under them. 50. The wall plates to upper floors can be kept clear of the walls on 3 in. rough quarried stone corbling built into the wall and projecting over $4y2$ in., and supported by two courses of brick oversailing, roughly splayed off to the shape of the plaster cornice which will cover them. The floor joists are thus kept clear of the wall and can be strengthened by solid strutting between the ends. 51. All wall-plates should be bolted down to the wall, and the bolts should be built in-

to the wall as shown in Fig. 306, and should be fitted with nut on top to bind down the plate. 52. Beams or roof trusses should not rest over openings. They should be placed with their ends in pockets in the wall, and resting on stone templates. 53. They should frame into girders with stub tusk tenons and oak pins, or, better, should hang in iron stirrups. 54. Binders should not be more than 6 ft., nor girders more than 10 ft. apart.

These general rules should be followed as closely as possible in the making of heavy timber roofs, but of course, must be changed or adapted to suit the many various conditions that are sure to arise.

There are many kinds or forms of roofs, a few of which I show in the sketches submitted which are original types. When these are crossed, mixed, modified or combined in one building or group of buildings, the results are not only beyond all computation, but are not unfrequently fearful and wonderful to behold.

To diminish the excessive height of roofs, their sharp summit is sometimes suppressed and replaced by a roof of a lower slope. These roofs have the advantage of giving ample attic space with a smaller height than would be required by a V-roof. They are variously known as "curb" or "gambrel" roofs, and "Mansard" roofs, the latter name being usually confined to those roofs in which tho lower slopes form angles of not less than 60 degrees with the horizontal plane, while roofs of smaller pitch are known as "curb" or "gambrel" roofs.

The Mansard roof may be described in several ways: (See Fig. 307.)

The triangle a d b, represents the profile of a high-pitched roof, the height being equal to the base, and the basal angles being therefore 60 degrees each. At the point e, in the middle of the height c d, draw a line horizontally h e i, parallel to the base a b, to represent the upper side of the tie-beam, and make e f equal to the half of e dj then a h f i b will be the profile of the Mansard roof.

Make c e, the height of the lower roof, equal to half the width a b, and construct the two squares adec, cegb; also make d h, e f, and g i each equal to one-third of the side of either squarej then will a h f i b, be the profile required.

On the base a b draw the semicircle a d b, and divide it into four equal parts, a e, e d, d f, f b; join the points of division, and the resulting semioctagon is the profile required. The slopes of the upper roof form angles of only 22% degrees, and this roof is therefore considerably less than ''quarter-pitch,'' and would be unsuitable for covering with slates, tiles, shingles, etc.

Whatever be the height of the Mansard c e, or b g, or g i, equal to the half of that height, and the height e f of the false roof equal to the half of e i. The upper roof, therefore, is exactly "quarterpitch."

The form of the Mansard roof, it will be seen, may be infinitely varied, according to the fancy of the designer, the purposes for which the roofspace is required, and the nature of the roof-covering. In many cases the lower slopes are made of curved outline, as may be seen later on, or as shown in No. 6, in the sketches.

It is now in order to give a few examples of a practical nature, and I will endeavor to do this without confusing the workman with a network of figures or mathematical formula: Like floors, roofs may be divided into three kinds, according to the arrangement of their timbering, as follows: 1. Single-Rafter Roofs.

2. Double-Rafter Roofs. 3. Triple-Rafter Roofs. 1. Single-Rafter Roofs are such that one roof covering is supported upon a single system of rafters not greater than two feet from center to center apart. It should be used only when the span is not greater than 26 feet. A number of examples of this kind of a roof are shown in Fig. 308. Other similar examples will be shown later on.

Lean-to roofs are found in a single slope, as shown at A, the upper end of the rafters being spiked to a wall-plate or bond timber supported on a corbel, and the lower end bird's-mouthed to a wall-plate on the lower wall. This roof should not be used for a span greater than 14 feet, unless the rafters are braced or otherwise supported near their centers. When a wall occurs conveniently near the center of the building, the roof may slope down towards the center, where a gutter or trough may be placed to carry off the rain or snow water. A double lean-to roof of this kind is sometimes called a V-roof, on account of the shape of its section.

Couple or span roofs are formed as shown at B, the upper ends of the rafters being abutted against and spiked to a ridge board, while the lower ends are either bird's-mouthed over and spiked to a wall-plate, or crow-footed over the outside of the plate and left projecting beyond the wall to form an eave for cornice. This form of roof should only be used on short spans unless the walls are thick and firm, or the rafters are tied at the bottom to keep from spreading, as an outward thrust is exerted by the feet of the rafters.

Couple close roofs are similar to the previous one, but have the feet of the rafters tied together by means of tie-beams fastened to the rafters, as shown at C Fig. 308. The soundest roof is procured by tying the feet of every pair of rafters, and indeed, this is necessary when a ceiling is to be attached to the ties; but when a roof is open a tie is rarely used more frequently than one for *Gable Roof with Pediment. Semicircular Arch Hoof. SuQgeetiom of Dormer Windows*

in Roofs.

9abls with Ornamented Verge-Boards. Queen Anns (or Mongrel f)

Plate No. 1.

every third or fourth pair of rafters. This roof may be employed for spans up to 30 ft. At C, a roof is shown over a span of 26 feet, but if larger roofs are to be constructed in this form the ridgeboard should be one inch deeper for every foot additional to the span. See Plates 1 and 2, "Types Of Roofs."

When the span is unusually great, it is more economical to suspend the ties to rafters, every six or eight feet. The ties between the bolts are housed into and spiked to a horizontal timber which is suspended by the bolts, as shown at D. When suspension bolts are used the depth of the ties may be half of that given in the foregoing rule.

Collar-beam roofs are formed like couple roofs with a beam or joist spiked or bolted to the rafters as shown at E. This type of roof is employed when a greater amount of head room is required than can be obtained in a couple-close roof, but it is not a sound roof, as it always exerts a thrust upon the walls. The collars being used to prevent the rafters from sagging, are in a state of compression, and do not tie the rafters together as they are generally supposed to *do*.

Double or Purlin roofs are composed of two series of timbers, as shown in Fig. 309, in which it will be seen that the roofs are composed of common rafters supported by means of purlins, for which reason this kind of roof is often called a purlin roof.

This sort of roof may be used for any span whatever when the gable walls are not too far apart, or when the rafters can be supported by studding from floor or central wall.

The outline of this roof, Fig. 309, shows it up as a "Mansard roof," the upper portion being practically a "couple-close" roof, the rafters resting upon purlins which are tied together by the ceiling joists, by bolts or heavy spikes. The lower rafters are practically independent of the upper portion of the roof, being merely bearers for the roof covering, and are secured by spiking them to the upper end of the purlin, and at the lower end to the wall-plate. The feet of these lower rafters do not need tying, as their inclination to the vertical is so small.

A couple of good purlin roofs suitable for many places, are shown in Figs. 310 and 311.

The one shown at Fig. 310 is known as a queen post truss, but having queen rods instead of posts. Two additional braces and one rod have been added to the members of the truss so as to take up the half load between the points F and H. According to the conditions of loading it has been formed sufficiently strong to bear all the load it may ordinarily be called upon to resist.

Taking the roof load first and assuming 40 pounds per square foot, including wind, snow and weight of roof itself, it is found that a load of about 7280 pounds will be concentrated at or near the points E and C. This load will cause a stress of about 13,500 pounds compression in each of the rafters A E and C B; also a compression strain of 11,300 pounds in the straining beam E C, as well as a tensile strain of about 11,300 pounds in the tie beam A B. In computing the strains due to the floor load, 200 pounds per square foot of floor area have been taken, including the weight of the flooring and the weight of the truss itself. The following table gives the strain on all the members of the truss due to both loads:

Pounds.

Main rafters A E and C B	65,450
Straining beam EC	41,800
Tie beam A B	55,050
Suspension rod D G	16,800
Braces DForDH	15,700
Rods E F or C H	28,000

These figures are, of course, only approximate, owing to the assumptions which have been made and the smallness of the diagram submitted, but they are of sufficient accuracy to draw the following conclusions: First, that the truss as shown in Fig. 310, is sufficiently strong to carry with entire safety the assumed loads here quoted, provided, however, the points of supports at A and B are sufficiently strong. From the diagram it appears as if the tie beam was tenoned into an upright post at each end and the parts pinned together. Con «idering the heavy load liable to be placed on a truss of this kind, it would seem doubtful whether this point is strong enough. In Fig. 311 I present a view of a truss in which an attempt has been made to improve on Fig. 310, using the same amount of material. It will be seen that the depth has been increased somewhat, which insures greater rigidity, and also gives the rafters less in clination to the horizontal, thus causing the strain to become less under the same load. It also affords better facilities for passing through the space between the members from one portion of the floor to the other. Again, the purlins rest directly on the trusses, thus doing away with the long 4x5 inch braces and also the short 7x7 inch posts. The small 4x4 inch braces shown in Fig. 310, can be dispensed with, as they receive no strains whatever.

The following diagram, Fig. 312, shows the elevation of a king-post roof suitable for a span of 35 or 40 feet.

By the rules for calculating the sizes of timbers the dimensions will be found to be as follows:

A, Tie-beam 13x5 inches.
B, Principal rafters 8%x5 inches.
C, Struts 4x2%. inches.
D, King-post.7%x5 inches.

Fig. 313 is the design for a king-post roof, for a span of from 40 to 45 feet.

The purlins here are shown framed into the principals, a mode of construction to be avoided, unless rendered absolutely necessary by particular circumstances.

The scantling, as determined by the rules, is as follows;

Principal rafters 10x5 inches.
Tie-beam Il%x6 inches.
King-post 7%x6 inches.
Struts 4x2% inchea
Purlins 10x6 inches.

The principals being 10 feet apart.

Fig. 314 shows a compound roof for a span of 40 feet. It is composed of a curved rib c c, formed of two thicknesses of 2-inch plank bolted together. Its ends are let into the tie-beam; and it is also firmly braced to the tie-beam by the king-post and suspending pieces B B, which are each in two thicknesses, one on each side of the rib and tiebeam, and by the straps a a. A is the rafter; d, the gutter-bearer; c and b, the straps of the kingpost. The second purlins, it will be observed, are carried by the upper end of the suspending pieces B B.

Fig. 315 shows a queen-post roof for a span of 60 feet. This truss is designed on the same principle as Fig. 311, that is, with queen-posts B, and additionally strengthened by suspension post A. These are strapped up to the tie-beam by wroughtiron straps, made of % by 3-inch iron, bolted tothe posts. The pitch of the principal rafter is less somewhat than over Fig. 311.

I *Fig.* 314.

The scantlings are as follows:

Principal rafters 11 x 6. inches
Tie-beam 12% x 6 inches
Queen-post B 8 x6 inches
Suspending-post A 3% x *3y2* inches
Struts (large) 4% x 3y2 inches
Struts (small) 3% x 2/2 inches

Figs. 316 and 317 show the use and application of wrought iron in those portions acting as ties. These trusses are suitable for railroad sheds, or where it is desirable to have the tie-rods raised from a level line so as to give greater height in the center. The sizes of timber for design 316 are as follows:

Principal rafters 12 x 8 inches
Struts 8 x 8 inches
Purlins 10 x 4 inches
Common rafters 4% x 2 inches
Tie-rod and suspending rod... *iy2* in. diameter.

The timbers for design 317 are as follows:

Principals 14 x 8 inches
Collar-pieces 11 x 3 inches (One on each side of rafter.)
Purlins 16 x 4 inches
Tie-rods and suspending-rod.. *1%* in. diameter.

The span of truss, Fig. 316, is 36, and that of Fig. 317, 45 feet.

Fig. 318 shows a platform roof of 35 feet span. The tie-beam in this example is scarfed at a and b, and the center portion of the truss has counterbraces, c c. The longitudinal pieces, e e, are secured to the heads of the queen-posts, and the pieces d carry the platform rafters A. In this connection it may be of importance to the better understanding of the principles of strength entering into combination roof trusses to give Tredgold's rules for finding the proper dimensions of the timbers forming king and queen-post trusses, which are quite simple.

Eule.—Multiply the square of the length in feet by the span in feet, and divide the product by the cube of the thickness in inches; then multiply the quotient by 0.96 to obtain the depth in inches.

Mr. Tredgold gives also the following rule for the rafters, as more general and reliable:

Multiply the square of the span in feet by the distance between the principals in feet, and divide the product by 60 times the rise in feet; the quotient will be the area of the section of the rafter in inches.

If the rise is one-fourth of the span, multiply the span by the distance between the principals, and divide by 15 for the area of section.

When the distance between the principals is 10 feet, the area of section is two-thirds of the span.

To find the dimensions of the tie-beam, when it has to support a ceiling only:

Rule.—Divide the length of the longest unsupported part by the cube root of the breadth, and the quotient multiplied by 1.47 will give depth in inches.

To find the dimensions of the king-post:

Rule.—Multiply the length of the post in feet by the span in feet; multiply the product by 0.12, which will give the area of the section of the post in inches. Divide this by the breadth for the thickness, or by the thickness for the breadth.

To find the dimensions of struts:

Rule.—Multiply the square root of the length supported in feet by the length of the strut in feet, and the square root of the product multiplied by 0.8 will give the depth, which, multiplied by 0.6, will give the thickness.

In a queen-post roof. To find the dimensions of the principal rafters:

Rule.—Multiply the square of the length in feet by the span in feet, and divide the product by the cube of the thickness in inches; the quotient multiplied by 0.155 will give the depth.

To find the dimensions of the tie-beam:

Rule.—Divide the length of the longest unsupported part by the cube root of the breadth, and the quotient multiplied by 1.47 will give the depth. To find the dimensions of the queen-posts: Rule.—Multiply the length in feet of that part of the tie-beam it supports; the product, multiplied by 0.27, will give the area of the post in inches;

and the breadth and thickness can be found as in the king-post.

The dimensions of the struts are found as before.

To find the dimensions of a straining-beam:

Rule.—Multiply the square root of the span in feet by the length of the straining-beam in feet, and extract the square root of the product; multiply the result by 0.9, which will give the depth in inches. The beam, to have the greatest strength, should have its depth to its breadth in the ratio of 10 to 7; therefore, to find the breadth, multiply the depth by 0.7.

To find the dimensions of purlins:

Rule.—Multiply the cube of the length of the purlin in feet by the distance the purlins are apart in feet, and the fourth root of the product will give the depth in inches, and the depth multiplied by 0.6 will give the thickness.

To find the dimensions of common rafters, when they are placed 12 inches apart:

Rule.—Divide the length of bearing in feet by the cube root of the breadth in inches, and the quotient multiplied by 0. 72 will give the depth in inches.

It may be well to note some practical memoranda of construction which cannot be too closely kept in mind in designing roofs.

Beams acting as struts should not be cut into or mortised on one side, so as to cause lateral yielding.

Purlins should never be framed into the principal rafters, but should be notched. When notched they.will carry nearly twice as much as when framed.

Purlins should be in as long pieces as possible.

Horizontal rafters are good in construction, and cost less than purlins and common rafters.

At Fig. 319 I show one of the principals of the roof of a church. The following are the dimensions of the timbers:

There are five principal trusses, placed 14 feet apart.

A, tie-beam, in two thicknesses, 14 x 10 inches. Principal rafters, 13 inches deep at bottom, 112 inches at top and *10y2* inches thick. The rafters bear on

oak abutment pieces 11 x *iy2* inches, bolted between the ties and to each other.

D, collar-beam, in two thicknesses, one on each side of the rafter, and notched and bolted, 12 x *5y2* inches each.

E, purlins. The two lower, 13 x *6y2* inches; the upper, *liy2* x *8y2* inches; notched on the rafters and bolted.

F, common rafters, *5y2* x *2y2* inches, and 13 inches apart.

The discharging posts between the bracket pieces and the stone corbel are of oak, 6 inches square.

The dimensions of the ironwork are as follows: King-rod, 1% in. square, with a cast-iron key piece at top. Queen-rods, 1% in. square, having solid heads at rafters and secured at foot by being passed through solid oak pieces k, placed between flitches of the tie-beam and securely bolted, and there fastened with cast-iron washers and nuts.

Four bolts at abutment end of ties.... *iy2* in. sq. Two bolts at each oak piece, for suspending rods % in. sq.

Two bolts at each end of oollar-beam. . % in. sq.

Purlin bolts % in. sq.

The following example, Fig. 320, is taken from Bell's Carpentry, and shows a strong roof, one that will suit admirably for a factory or machineshop where there is likely to be jars or shakes caused by the machines in motion, or the rolling in of heavy freight. This roof may have a span of fifty feet, or even more if necessary. The principal rafter is set back a foot from the end of the tie-beam to give room for the wall-plate; the rise of the roof is 5 inches to the foot. In framing roofs of this kind the supporting rods should be furnished before commencing the frame; for then the length of the short principal rafters and that of the straining beam can be regulated or proportioned according to the length of the rods. It is best, however, for the middle rod to be twice the length of the short ones, reckoning from the upper surface of the beam to the upper surface of the principal rafters, and allowing one foot more to each rod for the thickness of the beam, and the nut and washer. For example, the middle rod is 11 feet long and the short ones 6 feet each; which, after allowing 1 foot, as above mentioned, makes the length of the long one, above the work side of the beam, twice that of the short ones.

The length of the rod above the beam is the rise of the rafter, and the distance from the center of the rod to the foot of the rafter is the run of the rafter; the length of the rafter can, therefore, be found by the usual way.

To find the length of the straining beam, add the run of the short principal rafter to the lower end bevel of the long one; substract this run from the run of the long principal, and the difference will be half the length of the straining beam.

The bolsters under the ends of the tie-beams are of the same thickness as that, and about 5 feet long.

Figs. 321 and 322 exhibit designs of roofs in an improved style, particularly adapted to those of a great span, as they may be safely extended to a very considerable width, with less increase of weight, and less proportionate expense, than any of the older styles. The principle on which they are constructed is essentially,the same as that of the Howe Bridge. The braces are square at the ends, the hardwood blocks between them being beveled and placed as shown in the diagrams. Each truss of this frame supports a purlin post and plate, as represented.

These roofs are easily made nearly flat, and thereby adapted to metallic covering, by carrying the walls above the tie beams to any desired height, without altering the pitch of the principal rafters, which ought to have a rise of at least 4 inches to the foot, to give sufficient brace to the upper chord or straining beam.

Fig. 321 is represented with counter-braces; and Fig. 322 without them. The counter-braces do not add anything to the mere support of the roof, and are entirely unnecessary in frames of churches, or other public buildings, where there is no jar; but they may very properly be used in mill frames, or other buildings designed for heavy machin-ery.

The illustrations do not show the whole length of the roof, but enough of the construction is shown to enable the workman to design the whole truss.

Figs. 323, 324 and 325 exhibit three steep or gothic roofs suitable for small churches, chapels or similar buildings having from 40 to 45 feet span. Fig. 323 is built entirely of wood, and Fig. 324 is of wood strengthened with iron straps and bolts. Fig. 325 contains less wood than either of the two preceding examples, but is supported by iron rods and is decidedly the stronger roof of the three. Fig. 323 makes a neat, cheap and very simple plan, and is sufficiently strong enough for efficient service on any ordinary building having a span of not more than 35 or 45 feet.

Fig. 326, which shows an arched ceiling, may be formed of 2-inoh planks from 6 to 10 inches wide, which should be planed to a regular thickness and then wrought to the proper curve on the edges as shown. The forms thus made are laid one over the other, breaking all joints, and may be in two or more thicknesses, and then spiked or bolted together as may be desired. Intermediate forms of lighter and rougher material must be made to be placed between the finished arches to carry lath and plaster, and should be spaced so that their centers would be 16 inches apart. In Fig. 327 the arch should be formed from planks 3 inches thick and 12 inches wide and in three courses; have all joints broken or spliced and then well spiked or bolted together and may be fastened to the roof braces as shown. Intermediate arches or ribs will be required to carry lath and plaster, same as in' Fig. 326. Either of these roofs will answer quite well for a span from 65 to 70 feet between the supporting column.

Fig. 328 shows a cheaply made roof, and one that is suitable for small spans. This is sometimes called a scissor roof, because of the two main braces which tie the feet, collar beam and rafters together, cross in the center.

A different roof, and a very strong one, if the workmanship is good, is shown at Fig. 329. In this A A repre-sents the wall plates, which are 4 by 8 inches. B B is the bottom cord of truss, 6 by 8 inches in section. C C are truss rafters, also 6 by 8 inches in section. D is the top cord of truss of the same dimensions. E E shows the position of the second plates, which are 6 by 6 in. in size and are notched on to the truss rafters. F F are braces framed at the top into C C. Gr Or G are iron rods used in strengthening the truss. Each truss rafter is bolted at the foot to the cord. The trusses should be placed about 10 feet apart. The roof rafters should be about 22 inches between centers.

I show a very good truss in Fig. 330. This is not a costly roof, but is very strong if well made. D shows the king-post, A the principal, C the cross-beam, B the brace and E a supporting post.

Another king-post truss is shown at Fig. 331. This truss is quite easy to make and easy to understand. A is the principal, D the king-post and C the tie beam. This is suitable for a span of from 30 to 35 feet.

Fig. 332 shows a truss that may safely be used where the span does not exceed 50 or 55 feet.

The truss shown at Fig. 333 is quite suitable for a light structure of about 30 feet span. The purlin posts are dovetailed into the beam and keyed. This makes it a very solid and stiff roof, and one that may be depended upon to do good service.

Fig. 334 shows a little more than half of a composite roof. The rafters and struts may be made of pitchpine, and the king-bolt and ties of iron. The roof is to carry ordinary slating, and the trusses will be spaced 10 feet apart. No holes are bored in struts or rafters; and all the ironwork is such as can be forged from the bar and fitted by a country blacksmith. The foot rests on a stone template.

The hammer-beam truss is a type of open, timber roof, and it is shown in Fig. 335, the letters in which have the following references: P R, principal rafters; K P, king-post; C, collar; S S, struts; H B, hammer beam; U B, upper bracket or compass piece; L B, lower bracket; S T, stud. A hammer beam truss exerts considerable thrust, and, therefore, substantial walls and also buttresses must be provided. A thickness of 18 inches is little enough for sound work with a span of 33 feet, but possibly the walls may be somewhat lightened by setting the window openings in 14-in. panels and adding buttresses outside the piers.

Fig. 336 shows the finished hammer beam roof. It may be used in public buildings or for small churches or chapels, the trusses being placed 10 or 12 feet apart. AAA show the finishing on the timbers and B B the drop ornament. The two details, A and B, show the sections on a large scale.

The example shown at Fig. 337 is an illustration of the hammer beam roof over Westminster Hall, London, and is said to be the finest of its kind in the world.

Westminster Hall is sixty-eight feet wide between the walls, and two-hundred and thirty-eight feet long. It is forty-two feet high to the top of the walls, and ninety feet to the ridge of the roof. It is divided into twelve bays, which will accordingly average nineteen feet ten inches each. Con sequently each truss has to span, sixty-eight feet, and to carry, in addition to its own weight, the weight of slates, timbers, etc., necessary to roof in 2,684 feet of floor. The pitch or angle which the slope of the roof makes with the horizon is 52 degrees. The material employed was at one time believed to be chestnut, but is really English oak. The appearance of the two woods is so much alike that some uncertainty may well be pardoned. The date of the roof is A. D. 1397, so that it is now over five hundred years old. The timber is in good preservation and of large scantling; that is to say, large sectional area. The workmanship throughout is of great beauty and accuracy, and no extensive repair, so far as can be seen, has ever been found necessary. The principal rafter of each truss is of considerable strength. The collar is placed just half way up the rafter. The hammer beams receive the foot of the rafters at their extremity, and each projects rather more than a quarter of the

span from the wall, and has its ends beautifully carved with the figure of an angle carrying a crown. A strong post is carried up from the end of the hammer beam to the point where the collar and the principal rafters join. A timber, which may be called a wall-post, rises from a corbel far down the wall, and supports the under side of the hammer beam at the point where it leaves the wall, and a second post vertically above this supports the principal rafter. There is a strong and richly molded rib which acts as a bracket or strut, springing from the corbel just referred to, and framed into the hammer beam, near its free end. A second similar rib, rising from the hammer beam, supports the middle of the collar. All these pieces, except the principal rafter, are knit together hy a magnificent arched rib springing from the corbel from which the lowest carved rib starts, and framed to the hammer beam, the post on the back of that beam, the collar, and both the curved ribs. Above the collar a second collar is introduced, and a post connecting the two is added, while at the middle of the truss, a central post, something like a short king-post occurs. Between all these timbers there is a kind of a filling-in of mullions or small posts, the space between having ornaments at the heads. These, no doubt, perform quite as much the important structural duty of connecting every member of the great framework together, as they do the artistic duty of filling up the great outline with subordinate features which give scale to it, enable its vastness to be appreciated, and bring out the variety of its lines by their contrast with, the uniformity of the filling-in.

The usual longitudinal purlins, running from truss to truss, are employed here, and furnish support to the roof rafters. The purlins are themselves supported lengthways from the great trusses by braces. The middle purlin is supported by a beautiful arched rib springing from the post on the hammer beam. The upper purlin has a curved brace springing from the principal Tafter. The lower purlin has a curved brace springing from the back of the great curved

rib. Below this purlin occur the openings of the roof covering, which correspond with the great dormer windows, from which the hall receives a considerable portion of its light, but which are said not to have been part of the original design.

The fineness of the workmanship shows that every ornamental part is equally well wrought, and is designed with the greatest skill, and the most honest work possible was expended on its construction.

A hammer beam queen-post truss is shown at Fig. 338. This roof is quite effective, both as to design and construction and would answer admir ably for any building not more than 45 feet span.

A cheaply formed roof, and one well suited for country churches, is shown at Fig. 339; where the finish also for the Apse of the church is shown. For small churches in the country, having a seating capacity of from 150 to 400, this kind of a roof and finish is well adapted. While it shows a hammer heam roof, it is simply neither more nor less than a scissor constructed roof.

The examples given, I take it, are quite sufficient to enable any smart workman to design and construct almost any kind of an ordinary roof of the class shown, so I leave the subject of hammer beam roofs, and, as promised in earlier pages, to show and explain some forms of Mansard, curb or gambrel roofs.

The roof shown in Fig. 340 is a true Mansard, and one of the best designed roofs of the kind. It is suitable for a span of 35 or 40 feet.

The three sketches, A, B, C, shown at 341, give some idea as to the rule governing the designing of Mansard roofs. It will be seen that in each case a semicircle, drawn from the middle of the base line touches the five main points of the truss. There are cafees, however, where the rule cannot always be applied. A noted authority on timberwork objects to this style of roof as being ungraceful in form and causing loss of room as compared with the original roofs of high pitch; and further, on account of the difficulty of freeing the gutters from snow. It is also dangerous on account of its inflammability.

Fig. 342 shows a Mansard roof, having a parapet wall. This roof is suitable for a span of 30 feet, and owing to the setback from the coping on the parapet wall, has a good appearance.

For a span of from 16 to 20 feet, the roof shown at Fig. 343 would answer very well and prove quite economical, both as to material and labor.

A self-supporting curb roof is shown at Fig. 344, which, is intended for a long span extending 50 feet or more. This shows how a flat curb roof may be constructed. For a less span, a king-post may be used and the two queen-posts left out. Braces could run from the foot of the king-post to the break in the principals at B and shaped with iron as shown. As roller skating rinks are again coming in use, this truss might in some cases be used for covering same. However, I now leave Mansard roofs, and will give an example or two of roofs suitable for skating rinks or for similar purposes.

The roof shown at Fig. 345 is one that has been employed over a rink having a floor space of 60 x 150 feet, and dressing rooms and galleries on the sides. The trusses are placed 14 feet apart. The purlins are 2x6, and are set two feet apart. The rafters over the galleries are 2x4 inches, set 2 feet apart, and at the upper ends are spiked into the lower purlin which lies at the foot of the trusses. The tie-beam is spliced in the middle by bolting a 2 x 8 timber on each side. The braces at the foot of the truss are spiked on both sides. The roof is sheeted with ⅞-inch pine boards, nailed on to the purlins parallel with the rafters and covered with No. 26 iron roofing. The dimensions of the timbers are marked on the sketch.

A roof more pretentious is shown at Fig. 346, which has been in use for some time. It is a very economical structure and not difficult to construct: The building is 80 x 172 feet, outside measurements, affording a skating surface of 64 x 154 feet. The sills are of solid timber, 8x8 inches, Norwaypine. The foundation consists of stone piers

14 x 14 inches, 24 inches deep, and 18 inches in the ground. These are in eight rows, extending the entire length of the building, 6 feet apart. The piers under the arches are 24 x 24 inches in size, and are 36 inches deep. The joists of the skating floor are 2 x 10 inches in size, placed 16 inches between centers. They are 14 feet long, and lapped together and thoroughly spiked. The cords running from arch to arch on each side of the building the entire length to support the roof are of 4 x 10 timber properly gained into the principal rafters. From each arch to the outside studding a 2 x 8 inch tie is spiked. The building is covered with drop siding, from 6 inch C strips. The roof projects 6 inches, and is finished with a plain barge board and facia. The skating surface is covered with an under floor of common pine boards, surfaced and laid diagonally. These are nailed to the joists and are covered with felt. The skating floor is of dry, matched, clear maple flooring, y8 inch thick and 2% inches wide, blind-nailed on bearings and smooth-planed and sand-papered after laying. The maple floor was laid with mitered joints at the corners, and with a rectangular space 14 feet wide in the center. The floors in the galleries and of the platforms are of common pine matched. The roof is hipped back from the end walls, which are 26 feet 9 inches high to the first arch. The entire roof is covered with cement roofing. The building has nine arches, located as shown on plans. These are 33y2 feet high and measure in section 10 x 15 inches. The arches are built of 1 x 10 inch boards, planed and jointed, and fastened together with l0d. and 20d. nails. The feet of the arches are gained 2 inches into -the cross-sills. The opposite cross-sills are connected together by 2 x. 10 tie-joists.

A lattice truss may often be used over short spans, or even for greater spans if the timbers and lattice strips are made in proportion. The truss shown at Fig. 347 will do nicely for a 27 feet span. The lattice trusses may have a rise of 3 feet and radius of 36 feet and be placed 7 feet apart. The top and bottom members may be made up by two separate thick-

nesses of 7-in. by 1-in. breaking joint. The lattice bars may be about 2y2 in. , 1% in-and 3 feet apart, radiating as shown. The purlins should be 3 in. by 2 in. at 3 feet centers, and covered with % -in. boarding and tarred felt. Cross bracing 4% in. by % in. between trusses as shown. The following is the rule for obtaining the radius of roof principals of the wood lattice pattern. If the rise be made one-tenth of the span, the radius will be thirteen-tenths of the span.

Thus, 85-ft. span equals 8-ft. 6-in. rise and 110ft. 6-in. radius, but this would be a large roof for such a system. The lattices may be arranged so that center lines through the top and bottom apices are radial to the external curve, as shown in Fig. 340, or the lattices themselves may be drawn towards two points equal to span apart and half span below tie-beam, as shown in Fig. 349. The former has the better appearance, but the latter has more crossings where the lattices can be secured to each other to help in stiffening them. Galvanized corrugated iron forms a good covering for these roofs.

Sometimes this kind of a truss is used in bridge building, but since steel has become such a factor in structural work, the lattice bridge or roof is very seldom employed.

I

Wooden spires, turrets and towers of various kinds are still erected in many parts of the country, and a book of this kind would scarcely be complete if these framings were not mentioned: Fig. 350 shows the construction of a spire 85 feet high above the tie-beam, or cross-timber of the roof. This is framed square as far as the top of the second section, above which it is octagonal. It will be found most convenient to frame and raise the square portion first; then to frame the octagonal portion, or spire proper, before raising it; in the first place letting the feet of the 8 hip rafters of the spire, each of which is 48 feet long, rest upon the tie-beam and "joists of the main building. The top of the spire can, in that situation, be conveniently finished and painted, after which it may be raised half way to its place, when the lower portion can be finished as far down as the top of the third section. The spire should then be raised and bolted to its place, by bolts at the top of the second section at AB, and also at the feet of the hip rafters at CD. The third section can then be built around the base of the spire proper; or the spire can be finished, as such, to the top of the second sections, dispensing with the third, just as the taste or ability of the parties shall determine.

No. 2 presents a horizontal view of the top of the first section.

No. 3 is a horizontal view of the top of the second section, after the spire is bolted to its place.

The lateral braces in the spire are halved together at their intersection with each other, and beveled and spiked to the hip rafters at the ends. These braces may be dispensed with on a low spire.

A conical finish can be given to the spire above the sections, by making the outside edges of the cross-timbers circular.

The bevels of the hip rafters are obtained in the usual manner for octagonal roofs, as described in other pages.

In most cases the side of an octagon is given as the basis of calculation in finding the width and other dimensions; but in spires like this, where the lower portion is square, we are required to find the side from a given width. The second section in this steeple, within which the octagonal spire is to be bolted, is supposed to be 12 feet square outside; and the posts being 8 inches square, the width of the octagon at the top of this section, as represented in No. 3, is 10 feet 8 inches, and its side is 4 feet 5.02 inches.

The side of any other octagon may be found from this by proportion, since all regular octagons are similar figures, and their sides are to each other as their widths, and conversely their widths are to each other as their sides.

Another example of high spire is shown at Fig. 351, in a completed state. This is taken from "Architecture and Building," published by Wm. Cumstock, New York, and is a good example of a tall slim spire.

This spire is 111 feet 6 inches high above the plate, and the latter is 69 feet above the sidewalk. The total height from sidewalk to top of finial is 190 feet. The tower is of stone, 19 feet square, with buttresses as shown. The spire is a true octagon in section, and each of the eight sides is braced in the same way, with the exception of the lower panel, in which the bracing is omitted on four sides back of the dormers. Besides the bracing shown in Fig. 352 the spire was braced across horizontally at each purlin to prevent distortion in the octagon. At the top the eight hips are cut against a ten-inch octagon pole and bolted to it in pairs. This pole is 32 feet long and is secured at the bottom by bolting to 4 x 6 crosspieces, which are securely spiked to the hips. In the center of this pole is a li/2-inch iron rod, which forms the center of the wrought iron finial.

The lower end of each hip is secured to the masonry by 1%-inch bolts, 6 feet long. The plate extends the full length of each side of the tower and is bolted together and to the walls at the corners. A short piece of 6 x 6 timber is placed on top of the plate, across the corners, to receive the rafters on the corner sides of the octagon. The braces and purlins are set in 4 inches from the outer face of the hips to allow for placing 2 x 4 jack rafters outside of them. These rafters are not shown in the figure; they were placed up and down, 16 inches on centers, and spiked to the purlins and braces.

As may be seen from Fig. 351, the top of the tower is rather light for supporting such a high framework, and is moreover weakened by large openings in each side. It was, therefore, determined to transfer the thrust due to the wind pressure on the spire to the corner of the tower at a point just below the sill of the large openings. The manner in which this was done is shown by Fig. 353, which is a diagonal section through top of tower. The purlins C, C, Fig. 351, were made 6 x 10 inches, set on edge and securely bolted to the hips. From the center of these purlins on each of the four corner sides 6 x 10-inch posts were carried down into the tower, as shown in Fig. 353. These posts were secured at the bottom to 10 x 10-inch timbers, which were placed across the tower diagonally and solidly built into the corners. The bracing shown was used merely to prevent the posts from bucking. Only one pair of posts is shown in the figure. The effect of these posts is to transmit the entire wind pressure on the leeward side of the tower from the purlins C, C to the corners of the tower at the bottom of the posts. The tension on the windward side is resisted by the hip rafters and the bolts by which CO they are anchored to the wall. This spire has stood for five years, and no cracks have as yet appeared in the tower, although the l-inch rod in the wrought iron finial was slightly bent during a severe gale.

The elevation and plans of the framework of a French spire are shown at Fig. 354, the whole is so plain that a further description of it is unnecessary. This is a fine specimen of French timber work and is worthy of study.

The tower shown at Fig. 355 is an old example of New England timber work—the plans are shown at No. 2 and No. 3. The illustration shows clearly enough the construction as to render description unnecessary.

Fig. 356 shows the elevation of a round tower, and Fig. 357 the plan and framework of same. As this example is somewhat different to the foregoing ones, some explanations are required to make the drawings clear and understandable.

Referring to Fig. 357, let it be supposed that 1, 2, 3, 4, etc., represent the plan of the toVer and M P its rise. Strike the plan full size or to a scale as may be most convenient.

For laying out the plan or line of the plate, draw lines for the rafters, as 15, 26, 37 and 48. Directly above the plan draw the elevation, beginning with a straight line, as K 0, to represent the plate, and make it the same length as 37 of the plan. Raise the center line M P the height of the tower and join 0 P and K P, which will be the lengths for all the rafters. To obtain the horizontal pieces A, B, C, D, etc., to which the sheeting is nailed in the manner represented in Figs. 1 and 2, proceed as follows: Divide the height into as many parts as desired—in this case six, which requires five horizontal pieces between each pair of rafters. The exact length and cut will be given by striking out the sweeps shown on the plan. A better idea of the manner in which the roof is constructed will be gained from inspection of Fig. 356, which shows each stud, plate, rafter and sweep in proper position, also the covering boards nailed on half way round. To obtain the exact shape, length and bevel for the covering boards the following method is employed: Take P of Fig. 357 as a center, with K as a radius, and describe the arc K R. The distance from K to R represents one-half of the circle or plan of the tower. The distance from K to R may be divided into as many parts as desired. In this case it is divided into fifteen parts, thus giving 15 tapering boards, which cover one-half the tower. Lines drawn from P to the arc K R are the inside lines of the joints. To obtain the bevel of the jointed edges of the boards set a bevel at V, as shown in Fig. 356. In the plan shown the rafters are cut so as to fit against a block, X, shaped to suit the plan of the roof. This manner of butting the rafters against the block X saves the time and labor of cutting the side bevels on the rafters which would be necessary if the block was not employed. A turret roof is shown at Fig. 358, and explanations are given on the drawing in connection with the framing and construction of the whole work, all of which should be readily understood by the workman.

I show two examples of towers in Figs. 359 and 360, and as the timbers shown are figured it would be waste of space to lengthen our description.

With these examples I conclude on spires, towers and turrets, and will now endeavor to show and describe some examples of timber barns, and work of a similar kind. The illustrations shown are sufficiently clear to render lengthy description unnecessary. The sketch shown at Fig. 361 is intended to represent the end of a barn about 55 feet wide. The open space under the main floor may be left as a shelter for cattle, or it may be built in an excavation in a bank, f orming what is known as a "bank barn."

Fig. 362 shows another sketch of barn which is slightly different from the previous one. This may be used as a bank barn or otherwise.

The sketch shown in Fig. 363 will answer for a center bent in either of the previous examples, as it forms a good trass in assisting the swing beam in carrying the upper structure.

Fig. 364 shows the side of a barn 65 feet long. This framing will suit any length of barn, and may be covered by any kind of a framed roof of the usual style. The openings may be filled in with studs and braces, or may be covered in with heavy rolling doors.

The sketches shown at Figs. 365 and 366 are intended to apply to roofs having a span of not more than 40 feet. The roof shown at Fig. 365 lis nicely adapted for using a "hay fork," as the timber in the ridge-will accommodate the fork and its appliances.

I show a number of designs for framing barns with gambrel roofs at Figs. 367, 368, 369, 370, 371 and 372. These will, I think, be ample to meet almost any requirement in this class of roofs. Figs. 369 and 370 appear to be favorites with f ramers in some parts of the west where there are barns that have been built on these lines over thirty years ago, and which are still doing good service after "braving the battle and the breezes and cyclones" so long, and they still give promise of doing business at the old stands for many years yet to come.

Temporary seats, or "grand stands," for fairs, exhibitions, outside conventions or similar occasions, are often called for, and the man who knows how best and most economically to build same will be the man to secure the contract for such work.

While I do not intend to go deeply into this phase of timber framing, I deem it due to my

To build a temporary lot of seats where the space is limited between walls, the proposition is rather a simple one, as the framing may easily be erected and slightly attached to the walls, or, if the walls permit of it, timbers may be laid so that their ends may rest in the walls, and they may be supported through the center by a triangular framework, such as shown at Fig. 373, and the seating may be built on as shown in Fig. 374.

This shows the principles on which all stands of this kind are built. Sometimes the timber and planking are all spiked or nailed together. This is objectionable as in that case all the bearing strength of the frame must be on the nails or spikes, something that should not be. A wuch

Fig. 374.

better way would be to put the frame together with large screws or bolts, then the framework can be taken down without much injury to the material. If the seats are to have benches on them, and to be raised above the ground at the lower end the steps must be made wider to suit Lliese conditions, as shown at Fig. 375. If chairs to be used on the platform the steps should not be less than 2 feet 4 inches wide, each having the proper rise. The diagram shows how such steps can be formed with a minimum of both materials and labor.

Another manner of constructing these galleries is shown in Fig. 376. In this case the upper platform is left about 5 feet 4 inches wide, which leaves room enough for seating on the step and for people to pass to and fro between the wall and the rear of the people on the seat. The diagram shown at Fig. 377 has a much steeper pitch, and is built over a series of trusses. This admits of the lower portion of the truss being arched, which gives more headroom to the floor below. The treads or steps in this series are much narrower than those shown in previous examples. Fig. 378 shows a portion of a gallery having an arched ceiling and an ornamented panel in the angle which relieves the work and makes a good finish. Another scheme is shown in Fig. 379.

This is figured on the plan so there is no need of further explanation.

Two other examples are shown at Fig. 380. The principal B is notched on the wall-plate Gr, and also on the beam E; the tie is secured on the wallplate H and bolted to the principal. F is a beam serving the office of a purlin to carry the gallery joists; D is a strut; bb are the floors of the pews or seats; and ccc the partitions; C is a hammerpiece or bracket resting on the beam E and bolted to the principal B; its outer extremity carries the piece I, which supports the gallery front.

No. 2, Fig. 380, is another example of the trussed principal A D C E, resting on the wall plate H, and front beam E supports the beam K, which carries the gallery joists B; a a and b b are the floors and partitions of the seats.

In building stands of this kind, or designing same, nothing should be let go as "good enough" if there be anything at hand better. All timbers should be of the very best and the workmanship beyond suspicion. In no other structure is honest work and faithful adherence to good and strong construction more needful than in the building of temporary structures of this kind.

What a terrible thing it would be if, because of your carelessness, incompetency, or defect in materials used in the stand or gallery, the whole structure loaded with young children and lady teachers, was to give way and throw every one to the ground or next floor, causing, perhaps, the loss of many young lives and many bone fractures. See that the timber is sound, that every joint fits snug and tight. Be sure of your foundation; have the building well braced, and your sleep will not be disturbed by fear of the tumbling down of your framed work.

The framing of bridges for short and medium spans, particularly in country, villages and towns, will generally fall to the lot of the expert framer. The designing of these bridges will also be executed by the carpenter and framer; and knowing this, I would not be doing my duty to the country carpenter if I did not submit a number of diagrams herewith for his guidance.

The design for a simple cheaply made bridge, shown at Fig. 381, is quite suitable for a road bridge having a span of about 30 ft. The timbers shown under the main chord tend to strengthen the whole work. The long timbers running across the creek will require to be as long as the chords of the truss; they will rest on the-string pieces, and should be bolted down to them. They should be placed not more than 6 feet from center to center. The deck of the bridge should be made of good sound 3 inch plank. The iron rods used in truss should be not less than seven-eighths of an inch in diameter.

Another truss bridge is shown at Fig. 382, which is a trifle easier to build than the one just shown. This is for from 18 to 22 feet span. Sizes of timber are figured out on the diagram.

The design shown at Fig. 383 is a most excellent one for a span of about 20 feet. This bridge will carry an enormous load if skillfully built. The timbers are all marked with figures, giving sizes of stuff required. This bridge, with plenty of stringers in it, would carry a railroad train. For foot bridges, either of the designs shown would answer very well, with about half the timbers in them as described on the diagram.

A very strong truss is shown at Fig. 384, that is suitable for a span of 50 feet, or even a little more. A part of the deck floor is shown at B B, and the cross timbers appear at A, A, A. This makes a good substantial bridge for a roadway and is very popular in many country places.

The design shown at Fig. 385 is made for a span of 40 feet. This is also a good design for a general roadway.

Another good truss is shown in Fig. 386 and one which is intended for a span of 75 feet. The bridge is 12 feet wide between trusses. The stringers rest on the cross-ties or beams A. The floor consists of 2-inch plank nailed on the stringers. The braces butt against a block which is bolted to the chord with two bolts ⅞-inch in diameter. The heel of the brace is also fastened to the chord with two bolts of the same size. At the point B there are two pieces 6x12 inches, notched and bolted with two bolts at the top and bottom. There is only a common key splice in the center of the chord. I do not think this to be a very strong bridge for this span, but I would suggest that in making use of it, it should be limited to a span of not more than 65 feet.

The trussed bridge shown at Fig. 386y2, is heavy enough for a railway bridge, though it is not intended for that purpose, having been designed for a roadway where much heavy traffic passes over it. The illustrations, Figs. 387 and 388, clearly show the construction and sizes of the different parts. Where strength and stability are desired I would not recommend that the parts be made lighter than indicated. In addition to the elevation of the truss, a plan is shown of the roadway, including the cross-braces, floor beams and planking. The cross-braces are 3x12, the floor beams 6x12, and the planking 2x12, laid diagonally. Other necessary particulars are furnished by the drawings, as Fig. 338 shows a portion of the deck or platform.

Ths truss shown at Fig. 388 is for a span of about 72 feet. The illustration showing the construction requires no explanation other than to say that the rods and plates should be provided with cast-iron washers of such shape that all the nuts will fit square with the bolts. The washers at the angles of the main braces and upper curves are made to take both rods and to extend over the joint sufficiently to hold the brace. The bridge shown is 72 feet span, or 75 feet extreme length. It has a roadway 14 feet wide. This, on a much traveled highway would be better 16 feet wide. The bridge should be constructed with about 6inch spring. If oak timber is used in the construction of the bridge, the dimensions of the pieces may be somewhat reduced from what is shown on the drawing.

The bridge shown at Fig. 389, is a double strut bridge, and is a very strong one; would answer for a roadway where heavy traffic crossed. The two struts, CC, on each side of the center show how it is braced, as also do the struts DD, which add much to the stiffness of the work. A shows the stringer, while B shows the timber for abutting the long struts against.

Another bridge of nearly the same span is shown at Fig. 390. This is a simple example with one strut on each side of the center of each beam; A is the chord or beam, B the strut, and C the strainingpiece bolted to the beam. The rail above the beam is for protection only, and is not intended to bear any part of the load, although, if properly framed, it will be of service in this respect.

When the spans are too great to be bridged in this simple manner, some method of trussing must be adopted. With scarcely an exception, the examples of trussed bridges may be resolved into the following groups (391): 1. Trusses below the roadway, and exerting a lateral thrust on the abutments. 3. Trusses below the roadway, composed of timber arches with ties and braces, but dependent on the abutments for resistance to lateral thrust. 4. Trusses below or above the roadway, composed of timber arches with ties and braces, and exerting only vertical pressure on the supports. 5. Lattice trusses above the roadway.

I show a bridge at Fig. 392, having a span of over 100 feet, that is not, properly speaking, a truss bridge, and which is not very difficult of construction. This bridge was built more than fifty years ago by the celebrated Thomas Telford, C. E., and it is still doing good service; and may continue to do so for many years yet, if it gets good care.

I show at Fig. 393 a 100-feet span trussed bridge constructed on the lines of the Howe Truss. I also give some data for figuring on the strength of this bridge and the loads it will carry. The bridge is, of course, a compound structure of steel rods and timber beams, which will probably be best. The dead load may be taken for trial at 7 cwt. per foot run, and the live load will be, say 7 cwt. per foot run, making a total load of tons, or 35 tons on each truss. Assume the elevation to be as shown in

No. 1, then the frame diagram will be as shown in No. 2, and the stress diagram as shown in No. 3. It will be necessary also to ascertain the stresses when the first three bays only are loaded, as this puts the fourth bay under a diagonal compressive stress when there is no compression member in the required direction, which is met by the compression member 19-20 undergoing 2.2 tons tension. The frame diagram for this will be as shown in No. 4, and the stress diagram as shown in No. 5. The stresses may be measured off the diagrams, and the bridge will then want careful designing to suit the material employed.

In the illustration shown in Fig. 394 is represented an ordinary lattice bridge which may have any ordinary span from 50 to 125 feet. No. 8 is the elevation of the common lattice bridge; No. 9, a section of the same when the roadway is above the latticed sides; and No. 10, a section when the roadway is supported on the under side of the lattice. No. 11, plan of one of the latticed sides.

Although when first introduced the lattice construction at once obtained great favor from its simplicity, economy, and elegant lightness of appearance, yet experfence has shown that it is only adapted for small spans and light loads, unless fortified by arches or arch braces. When well constructed, however, it is useful for ordinary road bridges Where the transport is not heavy.

A lattice-truss is composed of thin plank, and its construction is in every respect such as to render this illustration appropriate. Torsion is the direct effect of the action of any weight, however small, upon the single lattice.

Fig. 395 exhibits an elevation and details for an improved "Steele" lattice and trussed bridge, which is intended for long spans. The example shown was built over a span of more than 200 feet. The arch shown in the work adds to the stability of the work very materially.

The details shown are self-evident and hardly require explanation.

In building a Howe truss, it is quite essential that the chords be arched or cambered. There are several ways of getting this camber, but the one recom-

mended by Prof. De Vol son Wood of Stevens' Institute, Hoboken, N. J. is perhaps, about the best. He says: "Camber may be accomplished in various ways. Having determined the length of the main braces for straight chords, if their length be slightly increased, beginning with nothing in the center and increasing gradually towards the ends, any desired camber may be secured. This will give an arch form." The result, in an exaggerated form, is shown in Fig. 396. The bolts shown are all supposed to radiate to the center of the arch.

The object of cambering a truss is to allow for any settlement which may occur after completion, and also to prevent the truss from deflecting below a horizontal line when taxed to its maximum capacity. Some engineers allow 1-inch camber for a span of 50 feet; 2 inches for 100 feet, etc., while some, depending on the accuracy of their work, allow only one-half this amount. By cambering tihe horizontal timbers it is manifest that they must be made longer than the straight line which joins their ends. The increase in length of the lower chords due to cambering would be so trifling that in ordinary practice it could be entirely disregarded. Not so, however, with the upper chord; the increase in length of this member would be quite an appreciable quantity, because the top chord is cambered to a curve which is concentric to the curve of the lower one.

,

Trautwine and other authorities give a rule for determining this increase when the depth, the camber, and the span are given, providing, however, that the camber does not exceed one-fiftieth of the span,

Increase= depth X camber X 8 span using either feet or inches in the calculations. By cambering the truss the distance between the suspension rods on the upper chords will necessarily be greater than the distance between the rods on the lower chords. The panels are not strictly parallelograms, the rods converging somewhat. By dividing the total increase in length of the upper chord by the number of panels in the truss we obtain the increase per panel.

This, of course, will effect the length of the braces, and great care should be taken to cut these to the proper length. Trautwine also gives a method for finding the length of the braces in cambered trusses, but while the method shown is practically correct, in so far as lines are concerned, yet it could not be applied very well in a timber truss, at least, not so well as the method shown previously.

It must be remembered, that in calculating strains in trusses, skeleton diagrams are used, and the lines composing these diagrams are generally taken or drawn through the axes of the various members. These lines usually meet at a common point of intersection as will be seen from the dotted lines in Fig. 397. But in practice these lines do not always thus meet. The method shown by Trautwine is that of finding the length of the hypothenuse AC of the right angled triangle ABC; and even were these axial lines to meet at a common point of intersection the rule would not apply on account of the angle blocks taking up part of the distance. The best way to get the length would be to lay out one panel full size.

I show, at Fig. 398, a diagram of a Howe truss complete. This will give an idea of the way in which these trusses are constructed. A theoretical description of these styles of truss would scarcely he in place in this treatise, because of the fact that the carpenter who does the framing has but little to do with the theory, and because of the other fact that there are a number of excellent treatises in the market.

Another branch of timber framing is that of "shoring and needling," which may be analyzed as follows:

A system of raking shores, Fig. 399, consists of from one to four inclined timbers ranged vertically over each other, their lower ends springing from a stout sole-piece bedded in the ground, and their upper ends abutting partly against a vertical plank secured to the face of the wall and partly against the "needles"—horizontal projections that penetrate the wall-plate and the wall for a short distance.

The needles are generally cut out of 3-inch by 4%-inch stuff, the entering end reduced to 3-inch by 3-inch for convenience in entering an aperture formed by removing a header from the wall. The shouldered side is placed upwards, and cleats are fixed above them into the wall-plate to strengthen their resistance to the sliding tendency of the 2 shore. They are preferably sunk into the plate at the top end as indicated by the dotted lines in Fig. 400.

The head of the raker should be notched slightly over the needle, as shown in the detail sketch, Fig. 400, to prevent its being knocked aside, or moving out of position in the event of the wall settling1 back.

The top shore in a system is frequently made in two lengths for convenience of handling, and the upper one is known as the "rider," the supporting shore being termed the "back shore."

The rider is usually set up to its bearing with a pair of folding wedges introduced between the ends of the two shores. (See Fig. 399.)

Fig-401.

Braces are nailed on the sides of the rakers and edges of wall-plate to stiffen the former.

The sole-piece is bedded slightly out of square with the rakers, so that the latter may tighten as they are driven up.

The shores should be secured to the sole-piece with timber dogs; and, when in roadways or other public places, it is wise precaution to fix several turns of hoop-iron around their lower ends, fixing these with wrought nails.

A system of flying shores, see Figs. 401 and 402, consists of one or more horizontal timbers, called

"dog shores," wedged tightly between two wallplates, secured to the surfaces of adjacent walls. The middle of the shore is supported by braces springing from needles fixed to the lower ends of the plates, and are usually counteracted by corresponding inclined braces raking from the upper ends of the plates.

An angle of 45 degrees is the best for these braces, and abutments for their ends are supplied by straining or

"crown" pieces secured to the beam.

Wedges are inserted between the straining pieces and the brace to bring all up tight.

When one shore only is used, the best general position to fix it is about three-quarters the height of the wall, but much depends upon the state of the walls, and the nature or position of abutments behind them.

Where opportunity offers, a complete system of horizontal shores framed and braced to each other, as shown in Fig. 402, is a much safer way to prevent any movement of walls than is a series of isolated shores, which, being erected by different gangs of men,' and necessarily under a more divided supervision by the foreman, are likely to display considerable differences in their thrust or resistance to the walls.

Approximate rules and scantlings for raking shores:

Walls 15 ft. to 30 ft. high, 2 shores each system.

Walls 30 ft. to 40 ft. high, 3 shores each system.

Walls 40 ft. and higher, 4 shores each system.

The angle of the shores 60 degrees to 75 degrees —not more than than 15 ft. apart.

Walls 15 ft. to 20 ft. high, 4 in. x 4 in. or 5 in. x 5 in.

Walls 20 ft. to 30 ft. high, 9 in. x 4% in. or 6 in. x 6 in.

Walls 30 ft. to 35 ft. high, 7 in. x 7 in. Walls 35 ft. to 40 ft. high, 6 in. x 12 in. or 8 in. x 8 in.

Walls 40 ft. to 50 ft. high, 9 in. x 9 in. , 50 ft. and upwards, 12 in. x 9 in.

Horizontal shoring: Spans not exceeding 15 ft.—principal strut 6 in. x 4 in. and raking struts 4 in. x 4 in.

Spans from 15 ft. to 33 ft.—principal strut 6 in. x 6 in. to 9 in. x 9 in.; raking struts from 6 in. x 4 in. to 9 in. x 6 in.

The manner of shoring the upper part of a building is shown in Fig. 403. Particulars are given on the illustration, rendering further explanation unnecessary.

Another class of framing I have not yet touched upon is that where a timber structure, such as a tank frame, or a frame for a windmill, is required, and where the four corners lean in towards the center; and I will now endeavor to supply this deficiency: A structure of this kind may be called a "truncated pyramid," that is, a pyramid with its top end cut away at some point in its height leaving a platform level with the horizon, but of course less in area than the base. Thus, if we suppose a timber structure having a base 20x20 feet square, and a deck or platform 12x12 feet square there will be a difference of 8 ft. between the base and platform, or the platform will be 4 feet less on every side than the base, but the center of the base area must be directly under the center point of the platform area. If the structure is 15 feet high, or any other height that may be determined on, the four corner-posts will act as four hips, and will be subject to the same constructional rules as hip rafters, with some modifications and additions to suit changed conditions.

Of the many methods employed of obtaining bevels for oblique cuts on the feet and tops of posts having two inclinations, (and there are many), I know of none so simple as the one I am about to describe, and which can be applied in nearly every case where timbers meet at or on an angle, as in the case of struts under purlins, or the junction of purlins under hip or valley roofs. It is extremely handy for finding the bevels required for odd shaped tapered structures.

Let Figs. 404 and 405, show respectively an elevation and a plan of a raking timber meeting at an angle with a vertical timber. To obtain the bevel shown in the elevation Fig. 404 from the point B, set out a line square with the raking timber and draw the rectangle equal in width to AB, in the plan. Fig. 405, the angle of the diagonal of this rectangle with the pitch of the raking timbers marked F, is the bevel of the bird's mouth with the side. To obtain the bevel from the plan Fig. 405, draw the line CD, and through B, draw CE, equal to BC, in Fig. 404; join CE, and the required angle, which is the same as shown in Fig. 404, is obtained. The bevel required for the side of the strut is

the angle made by the pitch of the strut marked C, in Fig. 404, which needs no explanation. Figs. 406 and 407, show respectively an elevation and a plan of a raking timber butting at an angle against a plank, the section of the raking timber being shown by the dotted lines ABCD, in the same figure; the line AD, being the required bevel, that is, the angle it makes with a line parallel to the edge of the raking part indicated in the figure by the bevel. To obtain the bevel from the plan, draw the dotted line CD, Fig. 406, at right angles to the upright edge of the timber, making the line CGr, in the plan Fig. 407, equal to CD, in Fig. 406; draw the dotted line CD, Fig. 407, and at right angles to it draw X, Y, and project the front G, to E, making the distance of E, from XY, equal to the distance DE, in the elevation, Fig. 406; with D as a center, and E as radius, describe the dotted arc until it meets the line XY, and continue it down at right angles to meet a line from G, drawn parallel to XY, in H; then join CHD, and the angle obtained is the bevel required.

Fig. 408, and 409, show respectively an elevation and a plan of timbers both meeting angleways, one of them raking. To obtain the bevel from the elevation, draw the line EF, at right angles to edge DB, and passing through A, making the distance EF equal to one side of the section AB indicated by the dotted lines in Fig. 408. Draw the line BF and the angle this line makes with a line parallel to the edge is the required bevel for the top surfaces of the raking part which is indicated in Fig. 408, by J.

A similar method is adopted in obtaining the lower bevel, marked K, Fig. 408. The bevels are obtained from the plan Fig. 409, in a similar manner to those in Fig. 407. Make the line HG, Fig. 409, equal to HB in Fig. 408, and continue it down to E at right angles to the side. Join EB and draw XY at right angles; at right angles to XY, project the point A to D, making the height of D, above XY equal to the height of A above HB in Fig. 408. With B as a center, and D as radius, describe the dotted arc down to XY, and continue it on at right angles to meet the line AF drawn paral-

lel to XY; the angle EFB is the bevel for the two upper surfaces, and the same as the bevel J in Fig. 408. To avoid confusion, the bevel for the lower surfaces is not shown in Fig. 409, but is found in the manner already explained.

Fig. 410, is a section of a purlin, showing the pitch of the roof X, and the level line Y. Fig. 411 is a plan of Fig. 410, with a portion of a hip or valley rafter, making an angle of 45 degrees added, which occurs when the pitch of both sides of the roof is the same. When the pitches are different, bevels for the purlin on both sides of the hip or valley must be found; the angle that it makes with the pitch in the roof in plan being the only angular datum required. The method of finding the cuts is as follows: After drawing the purlin as shown in Fig. 410, draw the plan as in Fig. 411, and through the Point A, draw line FG at right angles to the edge of the purlin; make FG-equal in length to AC, Fig. 410, and join CG, which will give the bevel for the wide side of the purlin. The bevel for the narrow side is found in a similar manner by drawing DE through B, making it equal to ABr Fig. 410, and joining AE.

Fig. 411 shows all the lines necessary for obtaining the bevels in Figs. 410 and 411, the indices corresponding.

The methods shown herewith for obtaining the bevels and cuts for raking timbers of various kinds are quite simple compared with some methods taught. They are not new, nor are they original, as they have been in use many years among expert framers and millrights, and have been published, once before now at all events; the present method of rendering, however, I am persuaded, will be found simple and easily understood.

In connection with obtaining bevels of timbers that are set with an inclination, having one end resting on a floor and the other end cut to fit against a ceiling, the timber lying with two of its angles in the direction of its inclination and the other two at right angles to them.

In that case the upper end of the timber would require to be cut with the same bevels as the lower end, only reversing the bevels as both top and bottom bevels are alike.

If we consider the corner post as a prism, having four sides at right angles to each other, then when we cut the foot of it so obliquely a bevel as at ABC, Fig. 412, as to pitch it at the required inclination, the section resulting will not be square but lozenge shaped, as shown at Fig. 412, and this, of course, would not stand over a square corner and have its sides to correspond with the face of the sills or plates, so make the post a prism so that its sides will conform to the face of the sills in the "hacking" of the post. The lines to shape the post correctly to meet this condition may be obtained in several ways, but by far the simplest is shown at Fig. 413, where the square is employed to show the amount of overwood to be removed. Let us suppose the sills to be halved together as shown at Fig. 414, taking no notice of the tenon and mortise which are shown in this diagram, and this will give us as a ground plan of the sills, Fig. 415, KK, showing the ends of the sills which project past the frame. The point E in Fig. 413 will correspond with the point E Fig. 415 when the post is in position, and the points C and D will correspond with C and D in the same figure. To get the lines for the "backing" draw the diagonal line AB, on Fig. 413 then place the heel of the square on the line AB, near the long corner, and adjust the square on the timber so that the blade just coincides with the corner C, then mark along the blade and tongue of the square, continuing to G and H, and these points will be the gauge points sought, showing the slabs to be removed—DG and HC.

In laying off the bevels at the foot or top of the post, it must be remembered that the outside corners of the post, AA, Fig. 413 and 415, is the working edge from which the bevels must first be taken, so when the proper bevel is obtained, either by the square or by an ordinary bevel, we must proceed as follows: Bevel over from the corner A, first on one face of the post, then on the other; then turn the timber over and continue

the line across the next face to the corner, and perform the same operation on the fourth face. The lines are now complete for cutting the shoulders, but should there be a tenon on the post and a toed shoulder as shown at Fig. 414, then provision must be made for same, a matter the intelligent workman will find no difficulty in dealing with.

We will now deal with the bevels of the girts that are usually framed in between the posts of tapering structures. When the post only inclines in one direction, the problem of getting the bevels is a very simple one, as only the angle of inclination is required for the down cuts, the cross cuts all being square. With posts having two inclinations, how ever, the case is more complex and requires a different treatment, as all the cuts are bevels. While it is always—or nearly so—necessary to "back" the post on the outside, it is hardly ever necessary to perform a similar process on the inside corners of the post, therefore provision must be made on the shoulder of the girt to meet the condition, and this is done by cutting the shoulder on a bevel on both down and cross cuts. Let us suppose EF in Fig. 416 to be the down cut, or the angle of inclination, marked on the girt ABCD, just as the line would appear in elevation. Then from E to G, on F, set off a distance equal to the width of timber used in the girt, which would be equal to DC. Square down from the point G as shown to H, connect EH, and this line will be the bevel for the face end of the girt. This line being obtained carry a line across the top of the girt corresponding with the inside face of the corner post, and to find this line we must operate as follows: Let Fig. 417 be a reproduction of Fig. 416, then we lay the blade of the square on the line EF, and supposing the girt to be 8 inches square, we move the square along until the point 8 on the tongue coincides with the corner of the timber, when the heel of the square will define the point G. From G square up, obtaining the point K. Square across from K to the point L, which is on the inner corner of the girt. From L set off a distance back from the

post equal to the thickness of the slab that would have been removed from the post, if backed inside, which mark off at M, and from this point draw a line to E; then ME will be the bevel of the cross cut over the girt.

I have dwelled on this subject at some length because of some of the difficulties that surround it, and which in these pages I have endeavored to simplify and explain. Tapered structures of the kind discussed, whether on a square or polygon plan, are always troublesome to deal with unless the director of the work is well versed in a knowledge of the principles that underlie the construction of such structures and this means, almost, an education in itself. I have not touched on the rules for obtaining the lengths and bevels of diagonal braces in structures of this kind, as I am persuaded the sharp workman, who masters the rules given herewith, will be able to wrestle successfully with the diagonal regular tapered work.

Sometimes an irregular tapered frame is built to serve the purpose of a regular tank frame, then some changes from the foregoing take place.

If we build two frames same as shown at Fig. 418, and stand them plumb, with their faces as the illustration shows, any distance apart, there need be no trouble in framing them or in tieing them together with girts, as the latter may be framed into the posts square, and the cuts or bevels for the posts and cross timber may readily be obtained from the diagram of the work. Should the two bents, however, be made to incline towards each other, new conditions arise, that make it more difficult to get the joints for the girts, and backing for the posts. When the bents draw or lean into each other the posts have a double bevel or pitch making it take the form of a hip and as the posts are slanted over to form the pitch on the other side, we find that the face side, No. 2, Fig. 419 will draw in from the face of the sill on the corner B. The amount the post will draw in can be determined by cutting the proper bevels on bottom of post and placing side No. 1 Fig. 419, flush with the bent sill, then square out

B to A on side No. 2. The distance AB is the amount the post will draw towards the center as the bents are slanted towards each other. This distance is nothing more or less than the backing of the hip, but the bents being framed one side on the principal of a common rafter and then leaned towards each other, forming hips at the corners, cause the backing to come all on one side as shown in Fig. 420. Side No. 2 is the side that has to be backed in order to stand flush with sill, and the amount to take off the outside corner is the distance AB. For the bevel across the top of girts and braces on side No. 2, 419, square across the post as AC, set off AB same as is shown at bottom of post, and connect BC. A bevel set with stock on line of post and blade on line BC will give the required bevel: blade gives cut. The backing is perhaps more easily explained by Fig. 420. Cut a section of post to required bevels on the bottom and place a steel square flush with side No. 1 and it will show plainly the amount of backing to be taken from outside corner as ABC. These lines will not do to set the bevel by for cutting the top and bottom sides of girts and braces because AC in Fig. 420 is on the bevel of the bottom cut of hip and therefore is greater than the thickness of the post. The cut for girts and braces is the thickness of post and the backing applied as shown in Fig. 419.

Lightning Source UK Ltd.
Milton Keynes UK
UKOW010944100113

204636UK00009B/93/P